Machine Learning with Python

Scikits, TensorFlow, and Keras for Predictive Modeling.

COPYRIGHT

© [2024] by All rights reserved.

No part of this publication may be reproduced, distributed, or transmitted in any form or by any means, including photocopying, recording, or other electronic or mechanical methods, without the prior written permission of the publisher, except in the case of brief quotations embodied in critical reviews and certain other noncommercial uses permitted by copyright law.

Contents

Chapter 1: Introduction to Machine Learning 4

Definition and Importance of Machine Learning ... 4

Types of Machine Learning: Supervised, Unsupervised, and Reinforcement Learning 6

Overview of Predictive Modeling 7

Introduction to Python and Its Ecosystem for Machine Learning 9

Chapter 2: Setting Up the Environment 12

Installing Python and Essential Libraries 12

CHAPTER 3: OVERVIEW OF SCIKIT-LEARN, TENSORFLOW, AND KERAS 16

Setting Up Jupyter Notebooks for Interactive Development 18

CHAPTER 4: BEST PRACTICES FOR CODE MANAGEMENT 22

Chapter 5: Introduction to Scikit-Learn 25

Overview of Scikit-Learn and Its Architecture 25

Key Features and Utilities of Scikit-Learn 27

Implementing Basic Machine Learning Algorithms 30

Chapter 6: Understanding and Implementing Model Evaluation Metrics 36

Importance of Model Evaluation in Machine Learning 36

Key Evaluation Metrics for Classification Models 38

Key Evaluation Metrics for Regression Models ... 40

Practical Implementation of Model Evaluation Metrics 42

Chapter 7: Data Preprocessing Techniques in Machine Learning 48

The Importance of Data Preprocessing 48

Common Data Preprocessing Techniques 49

Implementing Data Preprocessing Techniques Using Scikit-Learn 52

Handling Missing Values 52

Categorical Encoding 54

Feature Scaling 55

Outlier Detection and Treatment 56

Feature Engineering and Dimensionality Reduction 57

Chapter 8: Feature Selection and Engineering for Predictive Modeling 60

Understanding Feature Selection and Engineering 60

- Techniques for Feature Selection 61
- Feature Engineering Techniques 63
- Practical Implementation of Feature Selection and Engineering 65
  - Feature Selection Using Filter Methods 65
  - Feature Selection Using Recursive Feature Elimination 66
  - Feature Engineering Example 67
  - Binning Continuous Variables 68
- Chapter 9: Model Training and Hyperparameter Tuning 70
  - Understanding Model Training 70
  - The Role of Hyperparameters in Model Training 71
  - Implementing Model Training and Hyperparameter Tuning with Scikit-Learn 73
    - Model Training Example 73
    - Hyperparameter Tuning Example 75
    - Random Search for Hyperparameter Tuning .. 77
  - Advanced Techniques for Hyperparameter Tuning 79
- Chapter 10: Model Evaluation Techniques 82
  - The Importance of Model Evaluation 82

Common Evaluation Metrics for Classification Models..83

Common Evaluation Metrics for Regression Models..86

Implementing Model Evaluation Using Scikit-Learn..87

    Model Evaluation for Classification 88

    Model Evaluation for Regression 90

Cross-Validation Techniques..................................92

Chapter 11: Deployment of Machine Learning Models..94

    Understanding Model Deployment 94

    Common Deployment Strategies............................95

    Tools and Frameworks for Model Deployment....97

    Monitoring and Maintaining Deployed Models....99

Chapter 12: Building Scalable Machine Learning Systems 103

    The Need for Scalability in Machine Learning...103

    Key Components of Scalable Machine Learning Systems 104

    Implementing Distributed Machine Learning....107

        Data Parallelism vs. Model Parallelism...........107

Using Apache Spark for Distributed Machine Learning 108

Example of Distributed Training with PyTorch 109

Scaling Model Inference 112

Batch Inference 112

Model Optimization Techniques 113

Using a Model Serving Framework 113

Chapter 13: Advanced Techniques in Machine Learning 115

Introduction to Advanced Machine Learning Techniques 115

Ensemble Methods 116

Bagging (Bootstrap Aggregating) 116

Boosting 117

Deep Learning 117

Understanding Neural Networks 118

Convolutional Neural Networks (CNNs) 118

Recurrent Neural Networks (RNNs) 119

Transfer Learning 119

Pre-trained Models 120

Applications of Transfer Learning 120

- **Reinforcement Learning** 121
  - **Core Concepts in Reinforcement Learning** 121
  - **Popular Algorithms in Reinforcement Learning** 122
  - **Applications of Reinforcement Learning** 122
- **Unsupervised Learning Strategies** 123
  - **Clustering** 123
  - **Dimensionality Reduction** 124
  - **Anomaly Detection** 124
- **Chapter 14: Practical Applications of Machine Learning** 126
  - **Real-World Applications of Machine Learning** . 126
  - **Predictive Analytics** 127
    - **Finance** 127
    - **Healthcare** 127
    - **Marketing** 128
  - **Natural Language Processing (NLP)** 128
    - **Chatbots and Virtual Assistants** 128
    - **Sentiment Analysis** 129
    - **Language Translation** 129
  - **Computer Vision** 129
    - **Image Classification** 130

- Facial Recognition 130
- Autonomous Vehicles 130
- **Recommendation Systems** 131
  - E-Commerce 131
  - Streaming Services 131
  - Social Media 132
- **Robotics** 132
  - Industrial Automation 132
  - Drones 133
  - Robotic Assistants 133

Chapter 15: Ethics and Fairness in Machine Learning 135

Understanding the Importance of Ethics in Machine Learning 135

Bias and Fairness in Machine Learning 136
- Types of Bias 136
- Assessing Fairness 137
- Mitigating Bias 138

Accountability in Machine Learning 139
- Establishing Clear Responsibilities 139
- Documentation and Traceability 140
- Addressing Unintended Consequences 140

- The Importance of Transparency 140
  - Explainability 141
  - Open Communication 141
  - Building Trust..141
- Fostering Ethical Practices in Machine Learning 142
  - Education and Training 142
  - Establishing Ethical Guidelines........................142
  - Engaging Diverse Perspectives 143
  - Collaboration and Regulation 143
- Chapter 16: Machine Learning in Industry............145
  - The Role of Machine Learning in Various Industries..145
  - Machine Learning in Finance...............................145
    - Risk Assessment and Fraud Detection..............146
    - Algorithmic Trading...146
    - Customer Service and Chatbots......................147
  - Machine Learning in Healthcare 147
    - Predictive Analytics for Patient Outcomes 147
    - Medical Imaging and Diagnostics 148
    - Drug Discovery and Development....................148
    - Personalized Medicine..148

Machine Learning in Manufacturing 149
   Predictive Maintenance 149
   Quality Control 149
   Supply Chain Optimization 150
Machine Learning in Retail 150
   Personalized Recommendations 150
   Inventory Management 150
   Customer Segmentation 151
Machine Learning in Transportation 151
   Autonomous Vehicles 151
   Traffic Prediction and Management 152
   Logistics and Route Optimization 152
Chapter 17: Future Trends in Machine Learning .. 154
Emerging Technologies and Innovations 154
Advancements in Deep Learning 154
   Transformers and Natural Language Processing 155
   Generative Models 155
   Explainable AI 156
Automated Machine Learning (AutoML) 156
   Simplifying the Workflow 156
   Integration with Business Processes 157

Improved Performance through Ensemble Learning 157

Integration with Other Technologies 157

Internet of Things (IoT) 158

Edge Computing 158

Blockchain and Data Integrity 158

Focus on Ethical AI 159

Addressing Bias and Fairness 159

Regulation and Governance 159

Human-Centered AI 160

Chapter 1: Introduction to Machine Learning

Definition and Importance of Machine Learning

Machine Learning (ML) is a subset of artificial intelligence (AI) that focuses on the development of algorithms and statistical models that enable computers to perform tasks without explicit programming. In simple terms, it allows machines to learn from data and improve their performance over time. This capability is particularly significant in today's data-driven world, where vast amounts of information are generated daily.

The importance of machine learning lies in its ability to analyze large datasets quickly and efficiently. Traditional programming methods often struggle to keep pace with the volume and complexity of modern data. In contrast, machine learning models can identify patterns and correlations within the data that might be missed by human analysts. This ability has made ML indispensable across various fields, from finance and healthcare to marketing and transportation.

Businesses leverage machine learning to gain insights, make informed decisions, and drive innovation. For instance, companies use ML algorithms for customer segmentation, fraud detection, predictive maintenance, and recommendation systems. In healthcare, ML aids in diagnosing diseases, personalizing treatment plans, and predicting patient outcomes. As industries increasingly adopt data-driven approaches, the demand for machine learning expertise continues to grow.

Furthermore, machine learning plays a pivotal role in advancing technology. From self-driving cars to voice-activated virtual assistants, ML algorithms are at the heart of many modern applications. The integration of machine learning into various technologies enhances user experiences and automates complex tasks, leading to increased efficiency and productivity.

The ongoing advancements in machine learning techniques and computational power are transforming how we interact with technology. As researchers develop more sophisticated algorithms, the potential applications of machine learning expand, paving the way for future innovations. Understanding the fundamentals of machine learning is essential for anyone looking to harness its power and apply it effectively in real-world scenarios.

Types of Machine Learning: Supervised, Unsupervised, and Reinforcement Learning

Machine learning can be broadly categorized into three main types: supervised learning, unsupervised learning, and reinforcement learning. Each type has its unique approach and application, catering to different kinds of problems and datasets.

Supervised Learning involves training a model on labeled data, which means that the input data is paired with the corresponding output. The goal is to learn a mapping from inputs to outputs so that the model can predict the output for unseen data. Supervised learning is commonly used for classification and regression tasks. For instance, in a spam detection system, the model is trained on emails labeled as "spam" or "not spam," enabling it to classify new emails accurately.

In supervised learning, algorithms such as linear regression, decision trees, and support vector machines are frequently used. The effectiveness of supervised learning hinges on the quality and quantity of the labeled training data. More data typically leads to better performance, but it also requires careful management to avoid issues like overfitting.

Unsupervised Learning, on the other hand, deals with unlabeled data. Here, the model attempts to find hidden patterns or intrinsic structures within the data without any prior knowledge of the outcomes. Common applications of unsupervised learning include clustering and dimensionality reduction. For example, clustering algorithms like K-means can group customers based on purchasing behavior, enabling businesses to target specific segments.

Unsupervised learning is particularly valuable in exploratory data analysis, where the aim is to uncover underlying trends and associations. Techniques such as Principal Component Analysis (PCA) and t-distributed Stochastic Neighbor Embedding (t-SNE) are employed to reduce dimensionality and visualize complex datasets. However, unsupervised learning can be challenging due to the lack of labeled outcomes, making it harder to evaluate model performance.

Reinforcement Learning is a unique paradigm that revolves around the concept of agents interacting with an environment to achieve specific goals. In this setting, an agent learns by taking actions and receiving feedback in the form of rewards or penalties. The objective is to learn a policy that maximizes the cumulative reward over time. Reinforcement learning has gained traction in fields like robotics, gaming, and autonomous systems.

One of the key distinctions of reinforcement learning is the exploration-exploitation trade-off. The agent must balance between exploring new actions to discover their potential rewards and exploiting known actions that yield high rewards. Techniques like Q-learning and deep reinforcement learning have been instrumental in advancing this field, enabling breakthroughs in applications such as AlphaGo, which defeated a world champion in the game of Go.

Understanding these three types of machine learning is crucial for selecting the appropriate approach for a given problem. Each type has its strengths and limitations, and the choice often depends on the nature of the data, the problem at hand, and the desired outcomes.

Overview of Predictive Modeling

Predictive modeling is a key application of machine learning that focuses on predicting future outcomes based on historical data. It involves creating a model that captures the underlying patterns in the data, enabling it to make forecasts about future events. Predictive modeling is widely used in various domains, including finance, marketing, healthcare, and manufacturing.

The process of predictive modeling typically begins with data collection and preprocessing. Raw data is often messy and may contain inconsistencies, missing values, or irrelevant features. Data preprocessing involves cleaning the data, transforming it into a suitable format, and selecting relevant features for the model. This step is critical, as the quality of the data directly impacts the model's performance.

Once the data is prepared, the next phase is model selection. Different algorithms can be employed based on the nature of the problem—classification, regression, or time-series forecasting. For instance, if the goal is to predict customer churn, a classification algorithm might be chosen, while a regression algorithm would be suitable for predicting sales revenue.

After selecting the model, it undergoes training using a portion of the data. The model learns to identify patterns and relationships within the training set, adjusting its parameters to minimize errors. This training process often involves optimization techniques to ensure that the model generalizes well to unseen data.

Model evaluation is a crucial step in predictive modeling. Various metrics, such as accuracy, precision, recall, and mean squared error, are used to assess how well the model performs on a validation dataset. This evaluation helps identify potential issues, such as overfitting, where the model performs well on training data but poorly on new data.

Once the model is validated, it can be deployed for making predictions on new data. Continuous monitoring and updating of the model are essential to maintain its accuracy over time, as data patterns may change due to evolving market conditions or other factors.

Predictive modeling not only helps organizations anticipate future events but also informs decision-making processes. By leveraging data-driven insights, businesses can optimize strategies, improve customer experiences, and enhance operational efficiency. As machine learning technologies advance, the capabilities of predictive modeling are expected to grow, opening new avenues for innovation and growth.

Introduction to Python and Its Ecosystem for Machine Learning

Python has emerged as the leading programming language for machine learning and data science due to its simplicity, versatility, and extensive ecosystem of libraries and frameworks. The language's readability makes it accessible for beginners while still powerful enough for experienced developers.

The Python ecosystem offers a plethora of libraries specifically designed for machine learning and data analysis. Notable libraries include NumPy for numerical computations, Pandas for data manipulation and analysis, Matplotlib and Seaborn for data visualization, and Scikit-Learn for traditional machine learning algorithms. These libraries provide essential tools for data preprocessing, model training, and evaluation, enabling practitioners to streamline their workflows.

NumPy, with its support for multi-dimensional arrays and a wide range of mathematical functions, serves as the foundation for many other libraries. Pandas, on the other hand, excels in handling structured data, allowing users to perform operations such as filtering, aggregating, and merging datasets efficiently.

Visualization is a critical aspect of data analysis, and Matplotlib along with Seaborn provides a powerful toolkit for creating a wide variety of plots and charts. Visualizations help convey insights clearly and effectively, making it easier to interpret data and communicate findings to stakeholders.

As machine learning gained traction, libraries like Scikit-Learn emerged, offering a comprehensive collection of machine learning algorithms and tools. It supports various tasks, including classification, regression, clustering, and model selection, with an easy-to-use API that simplifies implementation.

For deep learning, TensorFlow and Keras are the go-to libraries in the Python ecosystem. TensorFlow, developed by Google, provides a flexible framework for building and deploying machine learning models. Keras, which runs on top of TensorFlow, offers a high-level interface that simplifies the process of creating deep learning models. Together, these libraries have made deep learning more accessible to developers, researchers, and data scientists.

In addition to these libraries, Python's active community contributes to a wealth of resources, tutorials, and documentation that facilitate learning and problem-solving. The availability of open-source projects and collaborative platforms, such as GitHub, further enriches the ecosystem.

As the demand for machine learning expertise grows, Python remains at the forefront, empowering practitioners to harness the power of data. Its versatility and robust ecosystem make it an ideal choice for those looking to delve into machine learning, whether for academic research, industry applications, or personal projects.

Chapter 2: Setting Up the Environment

Installing Python and Essential Libraries

To embark on your machine learning journey, the first step is to set up your development environment. Installing Python is crucial, as it serves as the foundation for running various machine learning libraries. The most recommended version for data science is Python 3, as it includes enhancements and libraries tailored for modern applications. You can download Python from the official Python website. During installation, ensure that you check the box to add Python to your system's PATH, making it accessible from the command line.

Once Python is installed, the next step is to set up a package manager, which simplifies the installation of libraries. The most popular package manager for Python is **pip**, which comes bundled with Python installations. You can use pip to install essential libraries for machine learning. However, an even better option for managing libraries and environments is **Anaconda**. Anaconda is a distribution that includes Python, several essential libraries, and tools, along with its own package manager, **conda**.

Using Anaconda simplifies the installation process and allows you to create isolated environments for different projects. This is particularly useful when working on multiple projects that may require different versions of libraries. To install Anaconda, download the installer from the Anaconda website, run it, and follow the installation instructions.

After setting up Anaconda, you can create a new environment using the command line. For example, you can create an environment called "ml_env" with Python 3.8 by executing the following command:

lua
Copy code
```
conda create --name ml_env python=3.8
```

Activate your new environment with:

Copy code
```
conda activate ml_env
```

With your environment set up, you can begin installing the necessary libraries. Key libraries for machine learning include:

- **NumPy**: A fundamental package for numerical computing in Python, providing support for arrays and matrices, along with a plethora of mathematical functions.
- **Pandas**: A powerful data manipulation library that introduces DataFrames, making it easier to handle structured data, perform operations like filtering and grouping, and read/write data from various formats (CSV, Excel, etc.).
- **Matplotlib**: A comprehensive library for creating static, animated, and interactive visualizations in Python. It's widely used for plotting data and creating informative visual representations.
- **Seaborn**: Built on top of Matplotlib, Seaborn simplifies the process of creating visually appealing statistical graphics. It provides a high-level interface for drawing attractive and informative visualizations.
- **Scikit-Learn**: The go-to library for traditional machine learning algorithms, offering a simple and efficient tool for data mining and data analysis.

To install these libraries using pip, you can run the following commands in your terminal:

Copy code
```
pip install numpy pandas matplotlib seaborn scikit-learn
```

If you're using Anaconda, you can also install these libraries using conda with:

Copy code
```
conda install numpy pandas matplotlib seaborn scikit-learn
```

Once you've successfully installed the libraries, you can test your setup by opening a Python shell or Jupyter Notebook, importing the libraries, and checking their versions. This ensures that everything is correctly installed and ready for use.

CHAPTER 3: OVERVIEW OF SCIKIT-LEARN, TENSORFLOW, AND KERAS

The landscape of machine learning is vast, and choosing the right libraries is critical for success. Three of the most prominent libraries in Python for machine learning are Scikit-Learn, TensorFlow, and Keras. Each of these libraries has its unique strengths and use cases, catering to different aspects of machine learning.

Scikit-Learn is widely regarded as the foundational library for traditional machine learning in Python. Its simple and consistent API makes it accessible for beginners while offering robust functionality for advanced users. Scikit-Learn supports a wide range of algorithms for classification, regression, clustering, and dimensionality reduction. It also provides tools for preprocessing data, selecting features, and evaluating model performance.

One of the key advantages of Scikit-Learn is its integration with other libraries in the Python ecosystem, such as NumPy and Pandas. This compatibility allows users to seamlessly transition from data manipulation to model building. The library's extensive documentation and user community further enhance its appeal, making it an excellent choice for both newcomers and experienced practitioners.

Moving into the realm of deep learning, **TensorFlow** has emerged as one of the leading frameworks for building and deploying machine learning models. Developed by Google, TensorFlow offers flexibility and scalability, enabling users to build complex neural networks and deploy them across various platforms, including mobile devices and web applications. The library supports a range of applications, from image and speech recognition to natural language processing.

TensorFlow's architecture is designed for high performance, making it suitable for training large models on massive datasets. Its ability to leverage GPUs and TPUs accelerates computation, which is essential for deep learning tasks that involve large amounts of data. Additionally, TensorFlow offers tools for distributed computing, making it easier to train models on multiple machines.

Keras is a high-level neural networks API that runs on top of TensorFlow, simplifying the process of building deep learning models. Keras allows users to create and train neural networks with just a few lines of code, making it an ideal choice for those new to deep learning. It provides a user-friendly interface and abstracts much of the complexity involved in model building.

With Keras, users can quickly experiment with different architectures and hyperparameters, allowing for rapid prototyping and iteration. The library includes a wide range of pre-built layers, optimizers, and loss functions, making it easy to create customized models. Keras also supports both convolutional and recurrent neural networks, catering to various types of data and applications.

In summary, Scikit-Learn, TensorFlow, and Keras are integral components of the machine learning ecosystem in Python. Scikit-Learn excels in traditional machine learning tasks, while TensorFlow and Keras facilitate deep learning applications. Understanding the strengths and appropriate use cases for each library is essential for effectively tackling machine learning problems.

Setting Up Jupyter Notebooks for Interactive Development

Jupyter Notebooks have become a staple for data scientists and machine learning practitioners due to their interactive nature and ability to combine code execution, text, and visualizations in a single document. Setting up Jupyter Notebooks allows you to create a flexible environment for experimentation, exploration, and presentation of your machine learning projects.

To install Jupyter Notebooks, you can use pip or conda. If you're using Anaconda, Jupyter is included by default. To install it via pip, simply run:

Copy code
```
pip install jupyter
```

Once Jupyter is installed, you can start the notebook server by opening your terminal and typing:

Copy code
```
jupyter notebook
```

This command will launch a web browser, displaying the Jupyter dashboard where you can create new notebooks or open existing ones. To create a new notebook, click on the "New" button and select Python 3 from the dropdown menu.

Jupyter Notebooks support Markdown, allowing you to document your code and analyses in a clear and organized manner. You can add headings, lists, links, and images, making your notebooks not only functional but also visually appealing. This documentation is particularly useful for sharing your work with others or revisiting your projects later.

The interactive nature of Jupyter Notebooks enables you to run code cells independently, allowing for iterative development. You can write a piece of code, execute it, and immediately see the results. This feedback loop fosters experimentation, enabling you to tweak parameters and visualize outcomes in real-time.

For machine learning projects, you can leverage libraries like Matplotlib and Seaborn within Jupyter Notebooks to create visualizations. These visualizations provide valuable insights into data distributions, relationships, and model performance, enhancing your understanding of the underlying patterns in your dataset.

Jupyter Notebooks also support integration with various data sources, including CSV files, databases, and APIs. This capability allows you to load data directly into your notebooks, perform analyses, and build models seamlessly. You can also save your notebooks in different formats, such as HTML or PDF, making it easy to share your findings with others.

In summary, Jupyter Notebooks offer a powerful and interactive environment for developing machine learning projects. Their ability to integrate code, visualizations, and documentation makes them an indispensable tool for data scientists and practitioners. By setting up Jupyter Notebooks, you create a flexible workspace for experimentation and exploration in the world of machine learning.

CHAPTER 4: BEST PRACTICES FOR CODE MANAGEMENT

As you dive deeper into machine learning projects, adopting best practices for code management becomes crucial for ensuring maintainability, collaboration, and reproducibility. Poor code management can lead to confusion, errors, and difficulties in tracking progress. Here are some best practices to consider as you embark on your machine learning journey.

First and foremost, use version control systems, such as **Git**, to manage your code. Version control allows you to track changes, revert to previous versions, and collaborate with others more efficiently. Creating a repository on platforms like GitHub or GitLab enables you to share your work with others, receive feedback, and collaborate on projects. Familiarizing yourself with Git commands such as commit, push, pull, and branch is essential for effective version control.

Next, organizing your project structure is key to maintaining clarity. A well-structured project typically includes directories for data, source code, notebooks, and documentation. For example, you might create the following structure:

kotlin

Copy code
```
project_name/
│
├── data/
│   ├── raw/
│   ├── processed/
│   └── external/
│
├── notebooks/
│
├── src/
│
├── requirements.txt
│
└── README.md
```

The **data** directory can be further divided into subdirectories for raw, processed, and external datasets. The **notebooks** directory can contain Jupyter Notebooks for exploratory analysis, while the **src** directory houses

Chapter 5: Introduction to Scikit-Learn

Overview of Scikit-Learn and Its Architecture

Scikit-Learn, often abbreviated as sklearn, is one of the most widely used libraries in the Python ecosystem for machine learning. Developed by David Cournapeau and other contributors, Scikit-Learn aims to provide simple and efficient tools for data mining and data analysis. Its rich functionality and easy-to-use API make it a popular choice for both beginners and experienced practitioners.

At its core, Scikit-Learn is built on several foundational libraries, including NumPy, SciPy, and Matplotlib. This foundation allows it to handle large datasets efficiently and perform complex mathematical operations. The library is designed to work seamlessly with these packages, which is one of the reasons it has gained such popularity among data scientists.

The architecture of Scikit-Learn is modular, which enhances its usability. It comprises various components that can be easily integrated to create a complete machine learning workflow. The primary modules include:

1. **Datasets**: This module provides utility functions to load sample datasets or generate synthetic datasets. It includes commonly used datasets such as the Iris dataset and the Boston housing dataset, making it easy to experiment with different algorithms.
2. **Preprocessing**: This module contains functions for data preprocessing, such as scaling, normalization, and encoding categorical variables. Preprocessing is a crucial step in the machine learning pipeline, as it ensures that data is in a suitable format for model training.
3. **Feature Selection**: Scikit-Learn offers several techniques for selecting the most relevant features from the dataset. Feature selection helps improve model performance by reducing overfitting and enhancing interpretability.
4. **Model Selection**: This module includes tools for cross-validation and hyperparameter tuning, enabling users to evaluate different models and select the best one for their specific tasks. Techniques like GridSearchCV and RandomizedSearchCV facilitate systematic hyperparameter optimization.

5. **Algorithms**: Scikit-Learn supports a wide range of machine learning algorithms for classification, regression, clustering, and dimensionality reduction. Some of the most commonly used algorithms include logistic regression, decision trees, random forests, support vector machines, and K-means clustering.
6. **Metrics**: This module provides various performance metrics for evaluating model performance, such as accuracy, precision, recall, F1-score, and mean squared error. These metrics are essential for assessing how well a model is performing on unseen data.

Scikit-Learn's design philosophy emphasizes user-friendliness and accessibility. The library follows a consistent API structure, where most functions and classes share similar method names and parameters. This consistency makes it easier for users to switch between different algorithms and utilities without having to relearn a new interface.

The library is also highly extensible, allowing developers to create custom estimators and transformers. This flexibility enables users to tailor Scikit-Learn to their specific needs, making it a versatile tool in the machine learning toolkit.

Key Features and Utilities of Scikit-Learn

Scikit-Learn boasts a myriad of features that make it indispensable for machine learning practitioners. Understanding these features will enhance your ability to leverage the library effectively in your projects.

One of the standout features of Scikit-Learn is its comprehensive set of algorithms. Whether you're working on a classification problem, regression task, or clustering challenge, Scikit-Learn has an algorithm tailored to your needs. For classification, you can choose from algorithms like logistic regression, decision trees, random forests, and support vector machines. For regression tasks, options include linear regression, ridge regression, and lasso regression. This variety allows practitioners to experiment with different models and select the best one based on performance metrics.

Another critical feature is the built-in support for model evaluation and selection. Scikit-Learn offers various functions to evaluate model performance using techniques like cross-validation. Cross-validation helps mitigate overfitting by splitting the dataset into multiple training and validation sets. The library also provides utilities for hyperparameter tuning through GridSearchCV and RandomizedSearchCV, allowing you to systematically search for the optimal hyperparameters for your model.

Preprocessing is a fundamental aspect of machine learning, and Scikit-Learn provides a robust set of utilities for this purpose. Data preprocessing can include scaling features, normalizing data, and encoding categorical variables. The library offers classes like StandardScaler for standardization, MinMaxScaler for normalization, and OneHotEncoder for converting categorical features into a format suitable for machine learning algorithms. These preprocessing utilities help ensure that your data is in the right shape for effective model training.

Additionally, Scikit-Learn facilitates feature selection, which is crucial for improving model performance and interpretability. The library provides techniques like recursive feature elimination (RFE) and feature importance scores to help identify the most relevant features in your dataset. By focusing on the most impactful features, you can reduce dimensionality, enhance model accuracy, and simplify interpretation.

Scikit-Learn also includes a suite of utilities for working with pipelines. Pipelines allow you to streamline the process of data preprocessing, model training, and evaluation into a single workflow. This not only enhances code organization but also ensures that the same preprocessing steps are applied consistently during training and testing. The Pipeline class in Scikit-Learn allows you to chain together transformers and estimators seamlessly, simplifying the overall process.

Furthermore, Scikit-Learn supports various evaluation metrics that allow you to gauge your model's performance effectively. From classification metrics like accuracy, precision, recall, and F1-score to regression metrics like mean squared error and R-squared, these metrics provide valuable insights into how well your model performs. The availability of these metrics ensures that you can make data-driven decisions when evaluating and refining your models.

Lastly, Scikit-Learn has a robust community and extensive documentation. The library is continuously updated with new features, improvements, and bug fixes. The comprehensive documentation includes tutorials, examples, and explanations for each function and class, making it easier for users to navigate the library and apply it to their specific needs.

Implementing Basic Machine Learning Algorithms

Implementing basic machine learning algorithms using Scikit-Learn is a straightforward process, thanks to the library's intuitive API. This section will guide you through the steps of loading data, preprocessing it, training a model, and evaluating its performance using a simple example.

To illustrate this process, let's consider a common machine learning task: classifying the famous Iris dataset. The Iris dataset contains measurements of iris flowers, classified into three species: Setosa, Versicolor, and Virginica. It includes four features: sepal length, sepal width, petal length, and petal width.

The first step is to load the dataset. Scikit-Learn provides a convenient utility to load sample datasets directly. You can import the necessary libraries and load the Iris dataset as follows:

python
Copy code
```
import numpy as np
import pandas as pd
from sklearn.datasets import load_iris
from sklearn.model_selection import train_test_split
from sklearn.preprocessing import StandardScaler
from sklearn.ensemble import RandomForestClassifier
from sklearn.metrics import classification_report, confusion_matrix

# Load the Iris dataset
```

```
iris = load_iris()
X = iris.data  # Features
y = iris.target  # Target variable
```

In this code snippet, we import the required libraries and load the Iris dataset. The features are stored in X, while the target variable (species) is stored in y.

Next, we need to split the dataset into training and testing sets. This is essential for evaluating the model's performance on unseen data. We can use the train_test_split function from Scikit-Learn to accomplish this:

python
Copy code
```
# Split the dataset into training and testing sets
X_train, X_test, y_train, y_test = train_test_split(X, y, test_size=0.2, random_state=42)
```

Here, we allocate 80% of the data for training and 20% for testing. The random_state parameter ensures reproducibility.

Once the data is split, it's often beneficial to preprocess the features. For instance, feature scaling can help algorithms converge faster and improve performance. In this case, we'll use the StandardScaler to standardize the features:

python
Copy code
```
# Scale the features
scaler = StandardScaler()
X_train = scaler.fit_transform(X_train)
X_test = scaler.transform(X_test)
```

The fit_transform method computes the mean and standard deviation for the training data and scales it, while the transform method applies the same scaling to the test data.

Now that our data is prepared, we can proceed to train a machine learning model. We'll use the Random Forest classifier as our model:

python
Copy code
```
# Initialize and train the Random Forest classifier
model = RandomForestClassifier(n_estimators=100, random_state=42)
model.fit(X_train, y_train)
```

In this snippet, we create an instance of the RandomForestClassifier and specify the number of trees in the forest using the n_estimators parameter. We then call the fit method to train the model on the training data.

After training the model, it's time to evaluate its performance on the test set. We can use the model to make predictions and then generate a classification report and confusion matrix:

python
Copy code
```
# Make predictions on the test set
y_pred = model.predict(X_test)

# Evaluate model performance
print(classification_report(y_test, y_pred))
print(confusion_matrix(y_test, y_pred))
```

The classification_report function provides a comprehensive overview of precision, recall, F1-score, and support for each class, while the confusion matrix visualizes the model's performance across different classes.

This example demonstrates the straightforward process of implementing a basic machine learning algorithm using Scikit-Learn. By following these steps, you can apply similar techniques to a wide variety of datasets and algorithms, making Scikit-Learn an invaluable tool for machine learning practitioners.

Chapter 6: Understanding and Implementing Model Evaluation Metrics

Importance of Model Evaluation in Machine Learning

In the realm of machine learning, model evaluation is a critical phase that determines how well a model performs on unseen data. Without proper evaluation, one cannot ascertain whether a model is genuinely learning patterns or simply memorizing the training data, leading to overfitting. Understanding and implementing effective evaluation metrics is paramount, as they provide insight into a model's performance, guiding decisions for model refinement and selection.

Model evaluation helps in quantifying the accuracy of predictions, assessing model generalization capabilities, and ensuring that it meets the desired performance criteria. Evaluation metrics are not just numbers; they reflect the model's ability to solve the problem at hand, be it classification, regression, or clustering. This is particularly vital in real-world applications where model predictions can have significant consequences, such as in healthcare, finance, and autonomous driving.

Choosing the right evaluation metric is essential, as different metrics highlight different aspects of model performance. For instance, accuracy may be misleading in cases of imbalanced datasets, where a model can achieve high accuracy by predicting only the majority class. Hence, understanding various evaluation metrics allows practitioners to make informed choices that align with the specific goals of their projects.

Another key aspect of model evaluation is the potential for iterative improvement. By analyzing performance metrics, data scientists can identify areas for enhancement, such as feature engineering, model tuning, or data collection strategies. This iterative process is fundamental to achieving a robust machine learning solution that delivers reliable predictions.

Ultimately, effective model evaluation fosters confidence in deploying machine learning models into production, ensuring they can perform reliably in dynamic, real-world scenarios. By grasping the importance of model evaluation and its various metrics, practitioners can navigate the complexities of machine learning with greater clarity and effectiveness.

Key Evaluation Metrics for Classification Models

When dealing with classification tasks, several evaluation metrics are commonly used to assess model performance. Each metric offers unique insights into how well a model predicts different classes. Understanding these metrics is crucial for selecting the right one based on the specific characteristics of your dataset and problem domain.

Accuracy is the most straightforward metric, defined as the ratio of correctly predicted instances to the total number of instances. While accuracy is easy to understand and compute, it can be misleading in cases of imbalanced classes. For example, in a dataset with 90% of instances belonging to one class, a model that predicts only that class could achieve 90% accuracy, despite being ineffective for the minority class.

Precision, also known as positive predictive value, measures the proportion of true positive predictions among all positive predictions. It is particularly useful in scenarios where the cost of false positives is high. For example, in spam detection, predicting a legitimate email as spam (false positive) can result in lost important messages. Precision helps quantify how many of the predicted positive cases are actually correct.

Recall, or sensitivity, measures the proportion of true positive predictions among all actual positive instances. This metric is crucial when the cost of false negatives is significant. For instance, in medical diagnostics, failing to identify a disease (false negative) could have severe consequences. Recall focuses on capturing as many actual positives as possible, providing insight into a model's ability to identify the target class.

F1 Score is the harmonic mean of precision and recall, providing a single score that balances both metrics. The F1 score is particularly valuable when dealing with imbalanced datasets, as it ensures that both false positives and false negatives are taken into account. A high F1 score indicates that the model is performing well across both precision and recall, making it a reliable measure for many classification tasks.

ROC-AUC (Receiver Operating Characteristic - Area Under Curve) is another important metric, especially for binary classification problems. The ROC curve plots the true positive rate against the false positive rate at various threshold settings. The AUC score quantifies the overall ability of the model to discriminate between classes, with a score of 0.5 indicating no discrimination and a score of 1.0 indicating perfect discrimination. ROC-AUC is particularly useful in scenarios with imbalanced classes, as it provides a holistic view of the model's performance across different thresholds.

Understanding these key metrics empowers practitioners to evaluate their classification models more effectively. Selecting the appropriate metrics based on the problem context ensures that the evaluation reflects the model's true performance and aids in refining it for optimal results.

Key Evaluation Metrics for Regression Models

In regression tasks, the goal is to predict continuous outcomes rather than discrete classes. Evaluating the performance of regression models involves different metrics tailored to assess how well the predicted values align with the actual target values. Understanding these metrics is crucial for interpreting the effectiveness of regression models.

Mean Absolute Error (MAE) measures the average magnitude of errors in a set of predictions, without considering their direction. It calculates the average of the absolute differences between predicted and actual values, providing a clear indication of the model's performance. MAE is particularly useful because it is intuitive and easy to interpret, making it a commonly used metric in regression analysis.

Mean Squared Error (MSE) is another widely used metric that calculates the average of the squares of the errors. MSE emphasizes larger errors more than smaller ones, as the differences are squared before averaging. This property can be advantageous when larger errors are particularly undesirable. However, MSE is sensitive to outliers due to the squaring of errors, which can lead to inflated values in the presence of extreme predictions.

Root Mean Squared Error (RMSE) is the square root of the MSE and provides an error metric that is in the same units as the target variable. RMSE retains the sensitivity to larger errors seen in MSE but offers a more interpretable metric. RMSE is often preferred in practice, as it reflects the model's average prediction error in a way that aligns with the scale of the target variable.

R-squared (Coefficient of Determination) quantifies the proportion of the variance in the dependent variable that can be explained by the independent variables in the model. R-squared values range from 0 to 1, with higher values indicating a better fit. While R-squared is useful for assessing model performance, it does have limitations. It does not indicate whether the model is appropriate or if the relationships between variables are valid, making it necessary to complement R-squared with other metrics.

Adjusted R-squared modifies the R-squared value to account for the number of predictors in the model. It penalizes excessive use of predictors that do not contribute to improved model performance, providing a more accurate reflection of the model's explanatory power. Adjusted R-squared is particularly useful when comparing models with differing numbers of predictors.

By leveraging these key evaluation metrics for regression models, practitioners can gain valuable insights into the performance of their models. Selecting the appropriate metrics based on the specific regression task ensures that evaluations are meaningful and conducive to model improvement.

Practical Implementation of Model Evaluation Metrics

Implementing model evaluation metrics in practice is essential for understanding how well a machine learning model performs. Scikit-Learn provides a straightforward way to compute these metrics, enabling users to evaluate their models effectively. Let's walk through a practical example of evaluating a classification model using common metrics.

Suppose we have built a classification model using the Iris dataset, as previously described. After training our model, we can use Scikit-Learn's utilities to evaluate its performance. Here's how to implement some of the key evaluation metrics for our Random Forest classifier:

python
Copy code
```
from sklearn.metrics import accuracy_score, precision_score, recall_score, f1_score, classification_report, confusion_matrix

# Make predictions on the test set
y_pred = model.predict(X_test)

# Calculate accuracy
accuracy = accuracy_score(y_test, y_pred)
print(f'Accuracy: {accuracy:.2f}')

# Calculate precision
precision = precision_score(y_test, y_pred, average='weighted')
print(f'Precision: {precision:.2f}')

# Calculate recall
recall = recall_score(y_test, y_pred, average='weighted')
print(f'Recall: {recall:.2f}')
```

```python
# Calculate F1 Score
f1 = f1_score(y_test, y_pred, average='weighted')
print(f'F1 Score: {f1:.2f}')

# Print classification report
print(classification_report(y_test, y_pred))

# Print confusion matrix
print(confusion_matrix(y_test, y_pred))
```

In this code, we use various metrics from Scikit-Learn to evaluate our model. The accuracy_score, precision_score, recall_score, and f1_score functions calculate their respective metrics based on the true labels and predicted labels. The average='weighted' parameter ensures that we account for class imbalance by weighting the metrics according to the number of true instances for each class.

The classification_report function provides a comprehensive overview of precision, recall, F1-score, and support for each class, while the confusion matrix visually represents the model's predictions, highlighting true positives, true negatives, false positives, and false negatives.

For regression tasks, implementing evaluation metrics follows a similar structure. Suppose we have trained a regression model to predict housing prices. Here's how to compute some of the key regression metrics:

python
Copy code
```
from sklearn.metrics import mean_absolute_error, mean_squared_error, r2_score

# Make predictions on the test set
y_pred = model.predict(X_test)

# Calculate Mean Absolute Error
mae = mean_absolute_error(y_test, y_pred)
print(f'Mean Absolute Error: {mae:.2f}')

# Calculate Mean Squared Error
mse = mean_squared_error(y_test, y_pred)
print(f'Mean Squared Error: {mse:.2f}')

# Calculate Root Mean Squared Error
rmse = mean_squared_error(y_test, y_pred, squared=False)
print(f'Root Mean Squared Error: {rmse:.2f}')

# Calculate R-squared
r2 = r2_score(y_test, y_pred)
print(f'R-squared: {r2:.2f}')
```

In this example, we calculate the Mean Absolute Error, Mean Squared Error, Root Mean Squared Error, and R-squared for our regression model. These metrics provide valuable insights into how well the model predicts housing prices, allowing for informed decisions regarding model performance and improvements.

By implementing these evaluation metrics effectively, practitioners can gain a comprehensive understanding of their models, enabling continuous improvement and refinement in their machine learning projects.

Understanding and implementing model evaluation metrics is essential for any machine learning practitioner. These metrics provide crucial insights into a model's performance, helping to gauge its effectiveness and guiding decisions for improvement. By leveraging the various metrics available in Scikit-Learn, practitioners can navigate the complexities of machine learning, ensuring their models are not only accurate but also reliable in real-world applications.

As you delve deeper into machine learning, continue to refine your understanding of evaluation metrics and their implications. The ultimate goal is to develop robust models that deliver value and insight, empowering data-driven decision-making in diverse fields. Embrace the iterative process of evaluation and refinement, as this is key to achieving success in your machine learning endeavors.

Chapter 7: Data Preprocessing Techniques in Machine Learning

The Importance of Data Preprocessing

Data preprocessing is a crucial step in the machine learning pipeline, significantly influencing the performance of predictive models. Raw data often comes in a form that is not directly suitable for analysis; it may contain missing values, outliers, and inconsistencies that can hinder model training. Effective preprocessing transforms this raw data into a clean, organized format that enhances the model's ability to learn patterns and make accurate predictions.

One of the main reasons preprocessing is essential is that machine learning algorithms operate on numerical data. However, real-world datasets often include categorical variables, text data, and various formats that need to be converted into a numerical representation. Additionally, data can be noisy or unstructured, which can confuse models and lead to poor performance if not addressed properly.

Another important aspect of preprocessing is feature scaling. Many machine learning algorithms are sensitive to the scale of the input features. For example, distance-based algorithms like K-Nearest Neighbors (KNN) and support vector machines (SVM) can be significantly affected if one feature has a much larger range than others. Scaling features ensures that all inputs contribute equally to the model, which can lead to improved convergence and performance.

Furthermore, effective preprocessing helps mitigate issues related to overfitting. By properly handling noise and irrelevant features, practitioners can create more robust models that generalize better to unseen data. This process also involves selecting relevant features through techniques such as feature engineering and dimensionality reduction, which can improve interpretability and reduce computational cost.

Overall, data preprocessing lays the groundwork for successful machine learning projects. By investing time and effort in cleaning and organizing data, practitioners set themselves up for better model performance, increased accuracy, and more reliable predictions.

Common Data Preprocessing Techniques

A variety of data preprocessing techniques are commonly employed in machine learning to prepare datasets for modeling. Each technique addresses specific issues and enhances the dataset's quality, allowing algorithms to learn more effectively.

1. Handling Missing Values: Missing data is a common challenge in real-world datasets. There are several strategies to handle missing values, including deletion, imputation, and interpolation. Deletion involves removing records with missing values, but this can lead to loss of valuable data. Imputation replaces missing values with estimates, such as the mean, median, or mode, while interpolation can fill gaps based on existing values. The choice of method depends on the extent of missingness and the dataset's characteristics.

2. Categorical Encoding: Many machine learning algorithms require numerical input, making it necessary to convert categorical variables into a suitable format. Common encoding techniques include one-hot encoding, which creates binary columns for each category, and label encoding, which assigns numerical labels to categories. Choosing the right encoding method is crucial, as it can impact model performance and interpretability.

3. Feature Scaling: Feature scaling is essential when dealing with algorithms sensitive to feature magnitude.

Standardization (z-score normalization) and Min-Max scaling are two common methods. Standardization transforms features to have a mean of zero and a standard deviation of one, while Min-Max scaling rescales features to a specific range, typically [0, 1]. Proper scaling can lead to faster convergence and improved model accuracy.

4. Outlier Detection and Treatment: Outliers can distort model training and predictions, so identifying and addressing them is critical. Techniques such as Z-scores, the Interquartile Range (IQR), and visualizations like box plots can help detect outliers. Depending on the context, outliers can be removed, capped, or transformed to reduce their influence on the model.

5. Feature Engineering: This process involves creating new features from existing data to improve model performance. Techniques include polynomial feature generation, interaction terms, and aggregating features. Feature engineering leverages domain knowledge to create more informative features that can enhance a model's predictive power.

6. Dimensionality Reduction: High-dimensional datasets can lead to overfitting and increased computational complexity. Dimensionality reduction techniques, such as Principal Component Analysis (PCA) and t-Distributed Stochastic Neighbor Embedding (t-SNE), help reduce the number of features while preserving essential information. This simplifies models, enhances interpretability, and improves generalization.

7. Data Normalization: Normalization involves transforming features to a common scale without distorting differences in the ranges of values. This is especially important for distance-based algorithms. Normalization techniques include min-max scaling and robust scaling, which uses the median and IQR to mitigate the influence of outliers.

Implementing Data Preprocessing Techniques Using Scikit-Learn

Scikit-Learn provides a robust set of tools for implementing various data preprocessing techniques, making it easier to prepare datasets for machine learning models. Let's explore how to implement some common preprocessing techniques using Scikit-Learn in a practical example.

Handling Missing Values

Suppose we have a dataset with missing values. We can use Scikit-Learn's SimpleImputer to handle these missing values effectively. Here's how you can implement it:

```python
import pandas as pd
from sklearn.impute import SimpleImputer

# Create a sample dataset
data = {
    'feature1': [1, 2, None, 4, 5],
    'feature2': ['A', None, 'B', 'C', 'A']
}
df = pd.DataFrame(data)

# Handle missing values for numerical and categorical features
numerical_imputer = SimpleImputer(strategy='mean')
df['feature1'] = numerical_imputer.fit_transform(df[['feature1']])

categorical_imputer = SimpleImputer(strategy='most_frequent')
df['feature2'] = categorical_imputer.fit_transform(df[['feature2']])

print(df)
```

In this example, we create a sample dataset with missing values in both numerical and categorical features. We use SimpleImputer to replace missing numerical values with the mean and categorical values with the most frequent category.

Categorical Encoding

Next, we can encode categorical variables using one-hot encoding. Scikit-Learn provides the OneHotEncoder class for this purpose:

python
Copy code
```
from sklearn.preprocessing import OneHotEncoder

# One-hot encode categorical features
encoder = OneHotEncoder(sparse=False)
encoded_features = encoder.fit_transform(df[['feature2']])

# Convert to DataFrame for better readability
encoded_df = pd.DataFrame(encoded_features, columns=encoder.get_feature_names_out(['feature2']))
df = pd.concat([df, encoded_df], axis=1).drop('feature2', axis=1)

print(df)
```

Here, we apply one-hot encoding to the categorical variable, creating binary columns for each category and dropping the original categorical column.

Feature Scaling

Feature scaling is essential for algorithms that are sensitive to feature magnitudes. We can use StandardScaler for standardization:

```python
from sklearn.preprocessing import StandardScaler

# Scale numerical features
scaler = StandardScaler()
df[['feature1']] = scaler.fit_transform(df[['feature1']])

print(df)
```

In this snippet, we standardize the numerical feature to have a mean of zero and a standard deviation of one.

Outlier Detection and Treatment

To handle outliers, we can identify them using the Z-score method and remove them from the dataset:

python
Copy code
```
import numpy as np

# Calculate Z-scores
z_scores = np.abs((df['feature1'] - df['feature1'].mean()) / df['feature1'].std())
df = df[z_scores < 3]  # Remove outliers with Z-score > 3

print(df)
```

Here, we calculate Z-scores for feature1 and filter out any rows where the Z-score exceeds 3, effectively removing outliers.

Feature Engineering and Dimensionality Reduction

Feature engineering involves creating new features from existing data. For dimensionality reduction, we can implement PCA:

python
Copy code
```
from sklearn.decomposition import PCA

# Assuming we have more features
```

```
pca = PCA(n_components=1)   # Reduce to 1 principal component
reduced_features = pca.fit_transform(df)

print(reduced_features)
```

This snippet reduces the dataset to a single principal component, allowing for dimensionality reduction while retaining essential information.

Data preprocessing is a vital component of the machine learning workflow that directly impacts model performance. By employing various preprocessing techniques, practitioners can ensure that their data is clean, organized, and suitable for model training. Leveraging Scikit-Learn's powerful tools simplifies the implementation of these techniques, allowing data scientists to focus on building effective models.

As you delve deeper into machine learning, understanding and mastering data preprocessing will be instrumental in achieving accurate and reliable predictions. Embrace the importance of preprocessing and the transformative power it brings to your machine learning projects.

Chapter 8: Feature Selection and Engineering for Predictive Modeling

Understanding Feature Selection and Engineering

Feature selection and engineering are pivotal processes in the machine learning pipeline that significantly affect model performance. Feature selection involves identifying the most relevant features in a dataset, while feature engineering focuses on creating new features from existing ones to enhance the model's predictive power. Together, these techniques help improve model accuracy, reduce overfitting, and increase interpretability.

The relevance of feature selection cannot be overstated. With high-dimensional datasets, many features may be redundant or irrelevant, introducing noise and complicating model training. Removing these extraneous features not only streamlines the dataset but also reduces the risk of overfitting, as models trained on fewer but more informative features can generalize better to unseen data.

Feature engineering complements selection by transforming existing features or creating new ones that encapsulate the underlying patterns in the data. This process is often domain-specific, relying on the practitioner's expertise to derive features that can lead to better model performance. By combining feature selection and engineering, practitioners can optimize their models, ensuring they capture the most critical aspects of the data while minimizing unnecessary complexity.

Ultimately, the goal is to enhance the predictive power of machine learning models. This requires a deep understanding of the dataset, the problem domain, and the algorithms being employed. By focusing on effective feature selection and engineering, practitioners can improve the robustness and accuracy of their predictive models, leading to more reliable and actionable insights.

Techniques for Feature Selection

Feature selection techniques can be categorized into three main approaches: filter methods, wrapper methods, and embedded methods. Each approach has its strengths and weaknesses, making them suitable for different scenarios.

1. Filter Methods: These methods assess the relevance of features based on statistical measures without involving any machine learning model. Common techniques include correlation coefficients, chi-squared tests, and mutual information scores. For example, the Pearson correlation coefficient can be used to identify linear relationships between features and the target variable. Features that do not show significant correlation can be eliminated, streamlining the dataset.

2. Wrapper Methods: Wrapper methods evaluate feature subsets by training a model and assessing its performance. Techniques such as forward selection, backward elimination, and recursive feature elimination fall under this category. These methods can yield better results than filter methods as they account for the interaction between features. However, they can be computationally expensive, especially with large datasets, since multiple models need to be trained and evaluated.

3. Embedded Methods: Embedded methods incorporate feature selection within the model training process itself. Algorithms like Lasso (L1 regularization) and decision trees inherently perform feature selection as part of their training. Lasso, for instance, encourages sparsity in the feature set by penalizing the absolute size of coefficients, effectively shrinking some coefficients to zero and eliminating those features from consideration.

Implementing feature selection effectively can lead to significant improvements in model performance, making it a critical step in the machine learning workflow.

Feature Engineering Techniques

Feature engineering is a creative process that involves transforming raw data into meaningful features that can enhance model performance. Several techniques can be employed in feature engineering, depending on the dataset and the problem at hand.

1. Creating Interaction Features: Interaction features capture relationships between variables that may not be apparent when examining them individually. For instance, if you have two features, age and income, creating an interaction feature like age_income_interaction = age * income can help the model learn complex relationships between these variables.

2. Polynomial Features: Polynomial feature generation allows for the modeling of non-linear relationships by creating polynomial combinations of existing features. For example, if x is a feature, creating x^2 or x^3 can help capture more complex patterns in the data.

3. Binning: Binning involves converting continuous variables into categorical ones by grouping values into discrete intervals. This technique can be particularly useful for capturing non-linear relationships. For example, you might bin ages into categories like young, middle-aged, and senior, which can make it easier for certain algorithms to learn from the data.

4. Log Transformations: Log transformations can stabilize variance and make the data more normally distributed. This is especially useful for skewed datasets. Applying a logarithm to a feature can help reduce the impact of outliers and improve model performance.

5. Feature Extraction: This technique involves deriving new features from existing data, particularly in unstructured data types such as text or images. For instance, using Natural Language Processing (NLP) techniques like Term Frequency-Inverse Document Frequency (TF-IDF) can convert text data into numerical features suitable for modeling.

6. Time-Series Features: When dealing with time-series data, extracting features related to time, such as day of the week, month, or seasonal trends, can enhance the model's ability to learn from temporal patterns.

By employing these feature engineering techniques, practitioners can create a rich set of features that encapsulate the underlying relationships within the data, leading to improved model performance.

Practical Implementation of Feature Selection and Engineering

In practice, implementing feature selection and engineering can be streamlined using libraries like Scikit-Learn and Pandas. Let's explore how to apply some of these techniques through a practical example.

Feature Selection Using Filter Methods

Suppose we have a dataset with several features, and we want to perform feature selection using correlation coefficients:

python
Copy code
```
import pandas as pd

# Load a sample dataset
df = pd.read_csv('data.csv')

# Calculate correlation matrix
correlation_matrix = df.corr()

# Select features with correlation above a threshold
```

```python
threshold = 0.5
relevant_features = correlation_matrix[correlation_matrix['target'] > threshold].index.tolist()

print(relevant_features)
```

In this example, we load a dataset and calculate its correlation matrix to identify features that correlate significantly with the target variable. We then filter the features based on a predefined correlation threshold.

Feature Selection Using Recursive Feature Elimination

For wrapper methods, we can implement Recursive Feature Elimination (RFE) with a linear model:

python
Copy code
```
from sklearn.linear_model import LinearRegression
from sklearn.feature_selection import RFE

# Separate features and target
X = df.drop('target', axis=1)
y = df['target']

# Create a linear regression model
```

```python
model = LinearRegression()

# Perform RFE
selector = RFE(model, n_features_to_select=5)
X_selected = selector.fit_transform(X, y)

print(X.columns[selector.support_])
```

Here, we utilize RFE to select the top five features based on the performance of a linear regression model.

Feature Engineering Example

Now, let's create interaction features and polynomial features using Scikit-Learn:

python
Copy code
```
from sklearn.preprocessing import PolynomialFeatures

# Create polynomial features
poly = PolynomialFeatures(degree=2, interaction_only=True)
X_poly = poly.fit_transform(X)

print(X_poly)
```

In this snippet, we generate polynomial features up to the second degree, focusing on interaction terms that capture relationships between features.

Binning Continuous Variables

To bin a continuous variable, we can use Pandas:

```python
# Bin a continuous feature into categories
df['age_bins'] = pd.cut(df['age'], bins=[0, 18, 35, 65, 100], labels=['child', 'young', 'adult', 'senior'])

print(df[['age', 'age_bins']])
```

This example bins ages into four categories, allowing the model to learn from these discrete age groups.

Feature selection and engineering are vital components of the machine learning process that can drastically improve model performance. By understanding and implementing various techniques, practitioners can enhance the predictive power of their models, reduce overfitting, and streamline the modeling process.

Using tools like Scikit-Learn and Pandas simplifies the implementation of these techniques, making it easier to prepare datasets for analysis. As you delve deeper into machine learning, mastering feature selection and engineering will empower you to create more robust and accurate predictive models, ultimately leading to better insights and decision-making. Embrace these practices as foundational elements in your machine learning journey.

Chapter 9: Model Training and Hyperparameter Tuning

Understanding Model Training

Model training is a fundamental step in the machine learning workflow, where the model learns patterns and relationships within the data. This process involves feeding the model a set of training data and adjusting its internal parameters to minimize the difference between its predictions and the actual target values. The effectiveness of this training process directly influences the model's performance on unseen data, making it crucial to implement it correctly.

During training, the model is exposed to input features and corresponding target labels. The objective is to find the best-fit parameters that minimize a loss function, which quantifies the discrepancy between predicted and actual values. Different types of machine learning models employ various algorithms to optimize their parameters. For instance, linear regression uses the least squares method, while neural networks utilize backpropagation and gradient descent techniques.

One important aspect of model training is the distinction between training, validation, and test datasets. The training set is used to fit the model, while the validation set helps tune the model's hyperparameters. The test set, which remains unseen during training, is crucial for evaluating the model's performance and ensuring it generalizes well to new data.

Choosing the right algorithm and appropriately training the model is critical for achieving optimal performance. Additionally, understanding the complexities of the training process allows practitioners to identify potential issues such as overfitting, where the model learns noise in the training data rather than general patterns.

By mastering the intricacies of model training, data scientists can develop robust models that deliver reliable predictions and insights across various domains.

The Role of Hyperparameters in Model Training

Hyperparameters are critical components of machine learning models that influence the training process but are not learned from the data. Instead, they are set before training begins and can significantly affect model performance. Hyperparameters include settings such as the learning rate, the number of trees in a random forest, or the architecture of a neural network.

Selecting appropriate hyperparameters is essential, as they control aspects of the learning process, such as the speed of convergence and the model's complexity. For instance, a learning rate that is too high may cause the model to converge too quickly to a suboptimal solution, while a rate that is too low can lead to excessive training times and inadequate learning. Similarly, in tree-based models, the maximum depth of trees can influence how well the model captures relationships in the data.

The process of tuning hyperparameters is often referred to as hyperparameter optimization. The goal is to find the best combination of hyperparameters that yields the highest performance on validation data. This process can be resource-intensive, especially when dealing with complex models and large datasets. However, it is crucial for enhancing the model's predictive capabilities.

Various techniques exist for hyperparameter tuning, including manual search, grid search, and random search. In manual search, practitioners adjust hyperparameters based on experience and intuition. Grid search evaluates all possible combinations of specified hyperparameter values, which can be exhaustive but computationally expensive. Random search randomly samples from hyperparameter space, often yielding competitive results with significantly less computation.

By effectively tuning hyperparameters, data scientists can unlock the full potential of their models, ensuring that they achieve the best possible performance on real-world tasks.

Implementing Model Training and Hyperparameter Tuning with Scikit-Learn

Scikit-Learn provides a user-friendly interface for model training and hyperparameter tuning, allowing practitioners to efficiently implement these processes. Let's explore how to train a machine learning model and perform hyperparameter tuning using Scikit-Learn through practical examples.

Model Training Example

For this example, we will use a simple dataset to train a Random Forest classifier. First, we will load the dataset, preprocess it, and then train the model.

```python
Copy code
import pandas as pd
```

```python
from sklearn.model_selection import train_test_split
from sklearn.ensemble import RandomForestClassifier
from sklearn.metrics import accuracy_score

# Load a sample dataset
df = pd.read_csv('iris.csv')

# Split the dataset into features and target
X = df.drop('species', axis=1)
y = df['species']

# Split into training and test sets
X_train, X_test, y_train, y_test = train_test_split(X, y, test_size=0.2, random_state=42)

# Train the Random Forest model
model = RandomForestClassifier(n_estimators=100, random_state=42)
model.fit(X_train, y_train)

# Make predictions on the test set
y_pred = model.predict(X_test)

# Evaluate the model's accuracy
accuracy = accuracy_score(y_test, y_pred)
print(f'Model Accuracy: {accuracy:.2f}')
```

In this code snippet, we load the Iris dataset, split it into training and test sets, and train a Random Forest classifier. We evaluate the model's performance by calculating its accuracy on the test set.

Hyperparameter Tuning Example

Next, we will perform hyperparameter tuning using Grid Search to find the best combination of hyperparameters for our Random Forest model. We will optimize parameters such as n_estimators (the number of trees) and max_depth (the maximum depth of each tree).

python
Copy code
```
from sklearn.model_selection import GridSearchCV

# Define the parameter grid for hyperparameter tuning
param_grid = {
    'n_estimators': [50, 100, 200],
    'max_depth': [None, 10, 20, 30]
}

# Initialize Grid Search
grid_search = GridSearchCV(estimator=model, param_grid=param_grid, cv=5, n_jobs=-1, scoring='accuracy')

# Fit Grid Search
```

```
grid_search.fit(X_train, y_train)

# Retrieve the best parameters
best_params = grid_search.best_params_
best_score = grid_search.best_score_

print(f'Best Hyperparameters: {best_params}')
print(f'Best Cross-Validation Accuracy: {best_score:.2f}')
```

In this example, we define a parameter grid specifying different values for n_estimators and max_depth. We then initialize GridSearchCV, fit it to the training data, and retrieve the best hyperparameters along with the corresponding cross-validation accuracy.

Random Search for Hyperparameter Tuning

In addition to Grid Search, we can also implement Random Search for hyperparameter optimization. This approach can be more efficient, especially with larger parameter spaces.

python
Copy code
```
from sklearn.model_selection import RandomizedSearchCV
```

```python
# Define the parameter distribution for Random Search
param_dist = {
    'n_estimators': [50, 100, 200],
    'max_depth': [None, 10, 20, 30]
}

# Initialize Random Search
random_search = RandomizedSearchCV(estimator=model, param_distributions=param_dist, n_iter=10, cv=5, n_jobs=-1, scoring='accuracy', random_state=42)

# Fit Random Search
random_search.fit(X_train, y_train)

# Retrieve the best parameters
best_random_params = random_search.best_params_
best_random_score = random_search.best_score_

print(f'Best Random Search Hyperparameters: {best_random_params}')
print(f'Best Random Search Cross-Validation Accuracy: {best_random_score:.2f}')
```

In this case, we define a parameter distribution for RandomizedSearchCV, which randomly samples from the specified hyperparameters. The results are similar to those from Grid Search, but with potentially less computational effort.

Advanced Techniques for Hyperparameter Tuning

Beyond Grid Search and Random Search, there are several advanced techniques for hyperparameter tuning that can lead to improved model performance and efficiency.

1. Bayesian Optimization: This probabilistic model-based approach seeks to find the minimum of a function in fewer iterations than grid or random search methods. Bayesian optimization builds a surrogate model to estimate the performance of hyperparameter configurations and uses it to guide the search process, making it more efficient.

2. Genetic Algorithms: Inspired by the process of natural selection, genetic algorithms evolve hyperparameter configurations over generations. They evaluate a population of configurations, selecting the best performers to create a new generation, combining and mutating parameters to explore the search space effectively.

3. Hyperband: Hyperband is a bandit-based method that dynamically allocates resources to different hyperparameter configurations based on their performance. It starts with a large number of configurations, evaluates them quickly, and iteratively eliminates the least promising ones, allowing for more efficient use of computational resources.

4. Optuna: Optuna is an open-source hyperparameter optimization framework that employs advanced techniques like pruning and optimization algorithms to efficiently explore the hyperparameter space. It allows for flexible and automated hyperparameter tuning, simplifying the optimization process.

Model training and hyperparameter tuning are integral components of the machine learning workflow that directly impact model performance. By understanding the training process and effectively tuning hyperparameters, practitioners can unlock the full potential of their models.

Scikit-Learn provides a comprehensive set of tools for implementing model training and hyperparameter tuning, making these processes more accessible to data scientists. As you continue your journey in machine learning, mastering these techniques will enable you to build robust and high-performing predictive models, leading to better insights and decision-making in various applications. Embrace the intricacies of model training and hyperparameter tuning as foundational elements in your machine learning toolkit.

Chapter 10: Model Evaluation Techniques

The Importance of Model Evaluation

Model evaluation is a critical step in the machine learning workflow, determining how well a model performs on unseen data. It involves assessing the model's accuracy, reliability, and generalization ability, ensuring it can make predictions that are consistent with real-world outcomes. Proper evaluation not only helps identify strengths and weaknesses in the model but also informs decisions about further improvements and refinements.

The primary goal of model evaluation is to ensure that the model is not overfitting or underfitting the training data. Overfitting occurs when a model learns the noise in the training dataset rather than the underlying patterns, leading to poor performance on new data. Conversely, underfitting happens when the model is too simplistic to capture the relevant patterns in the data, resulting in subpar performance even on training data.

To effectively evaluate a model, practitioners must employ a combination of metrics and techniques. The choice of evaluation metrics depends on the type of problem being solved—whether it is a classification, regression, or clustering task. For instance, classification tasks typically utilize metrics such as accuracy, precision, recall, and F1-score, while regression tasks rely on metrics like Mean Absolute Error (MAE), Mean Squared Error (MSE), and R-squared.

Furthermore, a comprehensive evaluation strategy incorporates techniques like cross-validation, which helps mitigate the risk of overfitting by assessing model performance across multiple subsets of the dataset. By dividing the data into training and validation sets multiple times, practitioners can gain a more robust understanding of model performance.

Ultimately, effective model evaluation is essential for developing trustworthy machine learning solutions. It provides the insights needed to make informed decisions about model selection, hyperparameter tuning, and feature engineering, paving the way for successful deployment in real-world applications.

Common Evaluation Metrics for Classification Models

When evaluating classification models, several metrics can be employed to assess performance. Each metric provides unique insights into different aspects of the model's predictive capabilities.

1. Accuracy: Accuracy is the simplest evaluation metric, representing the proportion of correct predictions made by the model out of the total predictions. It is calculated as:

$$\text{Accuracy} = \frac{\text{True Positives} + \text{True Negatives}}{\text{Total Predictions}}$$

While accuracy is a useful measure, it may not be the best choice in cases of class imbalance, where one class significantly outnumbers the other.

2. Precision: Precision, also known as positive predictive value, measures the proportion of true positive predictions among all positive predictions. It is particularly important in scenarios where false positives carry significant consequences. The formula is:

$$\text{Precision} = \frac{\text{True Positives}}{\text{True Positives} + \text{False Positives}}$$

3. Recall: Recall, or sensitivity, measures the proportion of true positive predictions among all actual positive instances. It is critical when the cost of false negatives is high. The formula is:

$$\text{Recall} = \frac{\text{True Positives}}{\text{True Positives} + \text{False Negatives}}$$

4. F1-Score: The F1-score is the harmonic mean of precision and recall, providing a balanced measure of a model's performance when there is class imbalance. It is particularly useful when you need to find a balance between precision and recall. The formula is:

$$\text{F1-Score} = 2 \cdot \frac{\text{Precision} \cdot \text{Recall}}{\text{Precision} + \text{Recall}}$$

5. ROC-AUC: The Receiver Operating Characteristic (ROC) curve illustrates the trade-off between true positive rates and false positive rates at various threshold settings. The area under the ROC curve (AUC) quantifies the overall ability of the model to discriminate between classes, with values closer to 1 indicating better performance.

Common Evaluation Metrics for Regression Models

For regression tasks, different metrics are employed to evaluate model performance, focusing on the accuracy of predicted continuous values.

1. Mean Absolute Error (MAE): MAE measures the average absolute differences between predicted and actual values, providing a straightforward interpretation of prediction accuracy. It is calculated as:

$$MAE = \frac{1}{n} \sum_{i=1}^{n} |y_i - \hat{y}_i|$$

2. Mean Squared Error (MSE): MSE computes the average of the squared differences between predicted and actual values, placing greater emphasis on larger errors. It is given by:

$$MSE = \frac{1}{n} \sum_{i=1}^{n} (y_i - \hat{y}_i)^2$$

3. Root Mean Squared Error (RMSE): RMSE is the square root of MSE, providing a measure of the average prediction error in the same unit as the original data. It is calculated as:

$$RMSE = \sqrt{\text{MSE}}$$

4. R-squared: R-squared, or the coefficient of determination, measures the proportion of variance in the dependent variable that can be explained by the independent variables in the model. It provides insight into how well the model fits the data, with values ranging from 0 to 1, where 1 indicates perfect prediction.

Implementing Model Evaluation Using Scikit-Learn

Scikit-Learn simplifies the implementation of model evaluation through built-in functions and classes that facilitate the computation of various metrics. Let's explore practical examples for both classification and regression tasks.

Model Evaluation for Classification

For this example, we will evaluate a Random Forest classifier using accuracy, precision, recall, and F1-score.

python
Copy code
```
from sklearn.datasets import load_iris
from sklearn.model_selection import train_test_split
from sklearn.ensemble import RandomForestClassifier
from sklearn.metrics import accuracy_score, precision_score, recall_score, f1_score, confusion_matrix

# Load the Iris dataset
data = load_iris()
X = data.data
y = data.target

# Split the dataset into training and test sets
X_train, X_test, y_train, y_test = train_test_split(X, y, test_size=0.2, random_state=42)

# Train the Random Forest model
model = RandomForestClassifier(n_estimators=100, random_state=42)
model.fit(X_train, y_train)
```

```python
# Make predictions on the test set
y_pred = model.predict(X_test)

# Evaluate the model's performance
accuracy = accuracy_score(y_test, y_pred)
precision = precision_score(y_test, y_pred, average='macro')
recall = recall_score(y_test, y_pred, average='macro')
f1 = f1_score(y_test, y_pred, average='macro')

print(f'Accuracy: {accuracy:.2f}')
print(f'Precision: {precision:.2f}')
print(f'Recall: {recall:.2f}')
print(f'F1-Score: {f1:.2f}')
print(f'Confusion Matrix:\n{confusion_matrix(y_test, y_pred)}')
```

In this snippet, we train a Random Forest classifier on the Iris dataset and evaluate its performance using various metrics. The confusion matrix provides additional insight into the model's classification performance across different classes.

Model Evaluation for Regression

For regression evaluation, we will assess a Linear Regression model using MAE, MSE, RMSE, and R-squared.

```python
from sklearn.datasets import load_boston
from sklearn.linear_model import LinearRegression
from sklearn.model_selection import train_test_split
from sklearn.metrics import mean_absolute_error, mean_squared_error, r2_score

# Load the Boston Housing dataset
data = load_boston()
X = data.data
y = data.target

# Split the dataset into training and test sets
X_train, X_test, y_train, y_test = train_test_split(X, y, test_size=0.2, random_state=42)

# Train the Linear Regression model
model = LinearRegression()
model.fit(X_train, y_train)

# Make predictions on the test set
y_pred = model.predict(X_test)

# Evaluate the model's performance
mae = mean_absolute_error(y_test, y_pred)
mse = mean_squared_error(y_test, y_pred)
```

```
rmse    =    mean_squared_error(y_test,    y_pred,
squared=False)
r2 = r2_score(y_test, y_pred)

print(f'Mean Absolute Error: {mae:.2f}')
print(f'Mean Squared Error: {mse:.2f}')
print(f'Root Mean Squared Error: {rmse:.2f}')
print(f'R-squared: {r2:.2f}')
```

In this example, we evaluate the performance of a Linear Regression model using various regression metrics, providing insights into the model's predictive accuracy.

Cross-Validation Techniques

Cross-validation is a powerful technique for assessing model performance, providing a more robust evaluation by using different subsets of the data for training and validation. This process helps mitigate the effects of data variability and provides a better estimate of the model's generalization capability.

1. K-Fold Cross-Validation: In K-fold cross-validation, the dataset is divided into K subsets, or folds. The model is trained K times, each time using K-1 folds for training and the remaining fold for validation. This process allows every data point to be used for both training and validation, providing a more comprehensive evaluation.

2. Stratified K-Fold Cross-Validation: This variation ensures that each fold maintains the same proportion of class labels as the entire dataset, making it particularly useful for imbalanced classification tasks.

3. Leave-One-Out Cross-Validation (LOOCV): In LOOCV

Chapter 11: Deployment of Machine Learning Models

Understanding Model Deployment

Model deployment is the final and crucial phase in the machine learning lifecycle, where a trained model is integrated into a production environment for real-world use. This process involves making the model available for predictions, ensuring it can accept new input data and return outputs efficiently. Successful deployment not only signifies the end of the development cycle but also the beginning of ongoing monitoring and maintenance.

Deploying a machine learning model involves several key considerations. First, practitioners must decide how the model will be accessed—whether through a web application, REST API, batch processing, or edge computing. The choice of deployment method often depends on the specific use case, performance requirements, and scalability considerations.

Moreover, the deployment environment plays a significant role in determining how the model will operate. This includes aspects such as hardware specifications, cloud infrastructure, and containerization options. For instance, deploying a model on cloud platforms like AWS or Azure can provide scalability and flexibility, while containerization with tools like Docker allows for easy distribution and environment consistency.

Monitoring the model post-deployment is essential to ensure that it continues to perform effectively. This involves tracking key performance metrics, validating predictions against actual outcomes, and implementing strategies for retraining the model as needed. As data changes over time, models can become outdated, necessitating regular updates and maintenance to maintain accuracy and relevance.

In summary, model deployment is a critical step that requires careful planning, execution, and monitoring. By understanding the intricacies involved in deploying machine learning models, practitioners can ensure that their models deliver value in real-world applications.

Common Deployment Strategies

There are several deployment strategies that practitioners can choose from, each offering unique benefits and challenges. The choice of strategy often depends on the specific requirements of the application, the target audience, and the nature of the model itself.

1. Batch Processing: In this approach, models are used to process large volumes of data at once, typically on a scheduled basis. This is ideal for scenarios where real-time predictions are not necessary, such as analyzing historical data or generating periodic reports. Batch processing can efficiently utilize resources, but it may not be suitable for applications requiring immediate feedback.

2. Online (Real-Time) Deployment: Online deployment allows models to make predictions in real time as data is received. This strategy is essential for applications that demand instant responses, such as fraud detection or recommendation systems. Online deployment often involves creating REST APIs that enable external applications to send data and receive predictions. While this approach provides immediacy, it requires robust infrastructure to handle varying loads and ensure low latency.

3. A/B Testing: A/B testing involves deploying multiple versions of a model concurrently to evaluate their performance against one another. This method allows practitioners to compare the effectiveness of different models or variations, helping to identify the best-performing option. A/B testing can provide valuable insights but requires careful implementation to avoid user confusion or disruption.

4. Canary Releases: This strategy involves deploying a new model to a small subset of users or data to monitor its performance before a full rollout. If the new model performs well, it can gradually be exposed to more users. This approach helps minimize the impact of potential issues and allows for easier rollback if necessary.

5. Containerization: Containerization, often facilitated by tools like Docker, allows models to be packaged with all their dependencies, making them portable and consistent across different environments. This approach simplifies deployment and scalability, enabling models to run seamlessly in various settings.

By selecting the appropriate deployment strategy, practitioners can effectively integrate their models into real-world applications, maximizing their impact and usability.

Tools and Frameworks for Model Deployment

Numerous tools and frameworks facilitate the deployment of machine learning models, providing capabilities for model serving, monitoring, and scaling. Below are some popular options:

1. Flask: Flask is a lightweight web framework in Python that is often used to create RESTful APIs for serving machine learning models. It allows for easy integration of model prediction functionality into web applications and is well-suited for prototyping and smaller projects.

2. FastAPI: FastAPI is a modern web framework designed for building APIs with Python 3.6+ based on standard Python type hints. It is particularly valued for its speed and automatic generation of OpenAPI documentation. FastAPI is ideal for deploying machine learning models that require high performance and asynchronous capabilities.

3. Docker: Docker is a containerization platform that enables developers to package applications and their dependencies into containers. This ensures consistency across different environments and simplifies the deployment process. Docker is commonly used in conjunction with model serving tools to create portable and scalable deployments.

4. TensorFlow Serving: TensorFlow Serving is a flexible, high-performance serving system for machine learning models designed for production environments. It provides capabilities for deploying TensorFlow models as well as other model types, allowing for easy integration and management of multiple models.

5. MLflow: MLflow is an open-source platform that manages the machine learning lifecycle, including experimentation, reproducibility, and deployment. It provides tools for tracking experiments, packaging models, and deploying them to various environments seamlessly.

6. AWS SageMaker: AWS SageMaker is a fully managed service that provides tools for building, training, and deploying machine learning models. It simplifies the deployment process and integrates with other AWS services, enabling scalable and secure model hosting.

7. Kubernetes: Kubernetes is a container orchestration platform that automates the deployment, scaling, and management of containerized applications. It is often used in conjunction with Docker to deploy machine learning models at scale, allowing for efficient resource management and load balancing.

By leveraging these tools and frameworks, practitioners can streamline the deployment process and ensure their models are effectively integrated into production environments.

Monitoring and Maintaining Deployed Models

Once a model is deployed, ongoing monitoring and maintenance are crucial to ensure it continues to deliver accurate predictions over time. As the environment, user behavior, and data change, models may experience performance degradation, necessitating regular evaluation and updates.

1. Performance Monitoring: Monitoring the model's performance involves tracking key metrics such as accuracy, latency, and resource utilization. By continuously assessing these metrics, practitioners can identify any anomalies or degradation in performance early on. Setting up alert systems can help notify the team of potential issues, allowing for timely intervention.

2. Drift Detection: Concept drift occurs when the statistical properties of the target variable change over time, impacting the model's performance. Implementing drift detection mechanisms can help identify when the model's predictions are no longer aligned with actual outcomes. Techniques such as monitoring prediction distributions, comparing current data against historical data, and employing statistical tests can aid in detecting drift.

3. Retraining Strategies: Regularly retraining the model on new data is essential for maintaining its performance. This can involve scheduled retraining, where the model is updated periodically, or on-demand retraining, which occurs when performance drops below a predefined threshold. Retraining ensures the model adapts to changes in the data distribution and remains relevant.

4. Versioning: Maintaining version control of deployed models is vital for tracking changes and facilitating rollbacks if issues arise. Tools like MLflow or DVC (Data Version Control) can help manage model versions, ensuring that practitioners can easily revert to previous iterations if necessary.

5. User Feedback and Iteration: Gathering user feedback on model predictions can provide valuable insights into model performance in real-world scenarios. Incorporating user input into the model's iterative improvement process can lead to enhanced accuracy and user satisfaction.

By implementing robust monitoring and maintenance practices, practitioners can ensure that their deployed models remain effective and reliable, ultimately delivering sustained value in real-world applications.

Model deployment is a critical phase in the machine learning lifecycle that involves integrating trained models into production environments for real-world use. Understanding deployment strategies, utilizing appropriate tools, and implementing effective monitoring and maintenance practices are essential for ensuring that models perform optimally and continue to provide value over time.

As the field of machine learning evolves, staying informed about the latest developments in deployment technologies and strategies will enable practitioners to successfully navigate the complexities of deploying models in diverse applications. By mastering the art of model deployment, data scientists can unlock the full potential of their machine learning solutions, paving the way for impactful and sustainable outcomes.

Chapter 12: Building Scalable Machine Learning Systems

The Need for Scalability in Machine Learning

As organizations increasingly rely on machine learning to drive decision-making, the demand for scalable solutions has never been greater. Scalability refers to the ability of a system to handle a growing amount of work or its potential to accommodate growth. In the context of machine learning, this means developing systems that can process larger datasets, serve more users, and respond to real-time demands without sacrificing performance.

Scalability is particularly important for several reasons. First, as the volume of data continues to grow exponentially, models need to be able to process this data efficiently. Large datasets often contain valuable insights that can enhance model performance, but they can also pose significant challenges in terms of computation and resource management.

Second, user expectations for responsiveness and real-time predictions are increasing. Applications that rely on machine learning, such as recommendation engines or fraud detection systems, require low-latency responses to remain effective and user-friendly. Therefore, deploying models that can quickly serve predictions under varying loads is crucial for maintaining a positive user experience.

Lastly, as organizations expand their operations or enter new markets, the need for scalable systems that can adapt to changing demands becomes essential. This adaptability ensures that machine learning models remain relevant and effective in diverse contexts, contributing to long-term success.

In summary, building scalable machine learning systems is vital for meeting the growing demands of data processing, user expectations, and organizational growth. By understanding the principles of scalability and implementing effective strategies, practitioners can develop robust systems that deliver reliable performance in real-world applications.

Key Components of Scalable Machine Learning Systems

Designing scalable machine learning systems involves several key components that work together to enhance performance and efficiency. Each of these components plays a crucial role in ensuring that the system can handle increased workloads and deliver timely predictions.

1. Distributed Computing: Distributed computing involves spreading computational tasks across multiple machines or nodes, allowing for parallel processing of data. This approach significantly enhances the system's capacity to handle large datasets and complex computations. Frameworks such as Apache Spark and Dask facilitate distributed data processing, enabling efficient model training and inference on massive datasets.

2. Data Storage Solutions: The choice of data storage solutions is critical for scalability. Traditional relational databases may struggle with the volume and velocity of data generated in machine learning applications. Instead, NoSQL databases (e.g., MongoDB, Cassandra) and distributed file systems (e.g., Hadoop HDFS) offer flexibility and scalability for storing unstructured data. Leveraging cloud storage solutions like AWS S3 or Google Cloud Storage can also enhance scalability by providing virtually unlimited storage capacity.

3. Microservices Architecture: Adopting a microservices architecture allows different components of the machine learning system to operate independently. This modular approach enables teams to develop, deploy, and scale individual services (e.g., data ingestion, model training, prediction serving) without impacting the entire system. By breaking down the monolithic architecture, organizations can improve agility and resilience.

4. Caching Mechanisms: Implementing caching mechanisms can greatly enhance the responsiveness of machine learning systems. By storing frequently accessed data or predictions in memory, systems can reduce latency and minimize the need for repetitive computations. Tools like Redis or Memcached can be utilized to manage caching effectively.

5. Load Balancing: Load balancing distributes incoming requests across multiple servers, ensuring that no single server becomes a bottleneck. This approach enhances system reliability and responsiveness, allowing for better handling of spikes in user demand. Load balancers can intelligently route requests based on server availability and performance, optimizing resource utilization.

6. Monitoring and Logging: Continuous monitoring and logging are essential for maintaining scalable systems. By tracking performance metrics and logging relevant events, organizations can identify potential bottlenecks or issues in real-time. This proactive approach allows for timely interventions and optimizations, ensuring consistent performance under varying loads.

By incorporating these key components into machine learning system design, practitioners can build scalable architectures that efficiently manage data processing and prediction serving.

Implementing Distributed Machine Learning

Distributed machine learning involves training models across multiple machines or nodes to leverage the power of parallel processing. This approach is particularly beneficial for large-scale datasets, allowing for faster training times and improved performance. Several techniques and frameworks facilitate the implementation of distributed machine learning.

Data Parallelism vs. Model Parallelism

When designing distributed machine learning systems, practitioners often choose between two primary paradigms: data parallelism and model parallelism.

Data Parallelism: In data parallelism, the same model is trained across different subsets of the data. Each node processes a distinct portion of the dataset, and the gradients from each node are aggregated to update the model parameters. This approach is effective when the model architecture is fixed and can benefit from larger training datasets. Frameworks such as TensorFlow and PyTorch support data parallelism, allowing users to scale their models across multiple GPUs or nodes seamlessly.

Model Parallelism: Model parallelism involves distributing different parts of the model across multiple machines. This approach is useful for very large models that cannot fit into the memory of a single machine. By partitioning the model, practitioners can leverage the computational power of multiple machines to train the entire model. However, model parallelism introduces additional complexity due to the need for communication between nodes.

Using Apache Spark for Distributed Machine Learning

Apache Spark is a widely used distributed computing framework that supports large-scale data processing and machine learning. It provides a high-level API for building scalable applications and integrates well with various data storage solutions. Spark's MLlib library offers a collection of machine learning algorithms that can be easily applied in distributed settings.

To implement distributed machine learning with Spark, practitioners typically follow these steps:

1. **Data Ingestion**: Load data from various sources into a Spark DataFrame. This may involve reading data from distributed file systems or databases.
2. **Data Preprocessing**: Perform necessary preprocessing steps such as data cleaning, feature extraction, and transformation using Spark's built-in functions.
3. **Model Training**: Train machine learning models using Spark's MLlib. Spark automatically distributes the training process across the cluster, leveraging the available resources.
4. **Model Evaluation**: Evaluate model performance using metrics that Spark provides. This can involve using cross-validation and hyperparameter tuning techniques.
5. **Model Deployment**: Once trained and validated, the model can be deployed using Spark Streaming for real-time predictions or integrated with other frameworks for batch processing.

Example of Distributed Training with PyTorch

PyTorch offers a simple way to implement distributed training through its Distributed Data Parallel (DDP) module. Here's a basic example:

python
Copy code
```
import torch
import torch.nn as nn
import torch.optim as optim
from torch.utils.data import DataLoader, DistributedSampler

# Initialize process group for distributed training
torch.distributed.init_process_group(backend='nccl')

# Define the model
class SimpleModel(nn.Module):
    def __init__(self):
        super(SimpleModel, self).__init__()
        self.fc = nn.Linear(10, 1)

    def forward(self, x):
        return self.fc(x)

# Create model instance
model = SimpleModel().to(torch.device('cuda'))

# Wrap the model with DDP
```

```python
model = nn.parallel.DistributedDataParallel(model)

# Define the optimizer and loss function
optimizer = optim.SGD(model.parameters(), lr=0.01)
loss_fn = nn.MSELoss()

# Load dataset and create a distributed sampler
dataset = YourCustomDataset()
sampler = DistributedSampler(dataset)
dataloader = DataLoader(dataset, sampler=sampler, batch_size=32)

# Training loop
for epoch in range(num_epochs):
    model.train()
    for inputs, targets in dataloader:
        optimizer.zero_grad()
        outputs = model(inputs)
        loss = loss_fn(outputs, targets)
        loss.backward()
        optimizer.step()
```

In this example, we set up a simple neural network and use PyTorch's Distributed Data Parallel to train the model across multiple GPUs or nodes. This allows for efficient training on larger datasets.

Scaling Model Inference

Scaling model inference is as crucial as scaling model training, particularly for applications requiring real-time predictions. Several strategies can be employed to ensure that machine learning models can serve predictions efficiently under varying loads.

Batch Inference

Batch inference involves processing multiple input samples simultaneously, allowing for more efficient utilization of computational resources. By grouping requests together, practitioners can reduce the overhead associated with serving individual predictions. This approach is particularly effective in scenarios where real-time predictions are not necessary, such as generating periodic reports or processing data in bulk.

Model Optimization Techniques

To enhance the performance of deployed models, practitioners can utilize various optimization techniques:

1. Model Compression: Techniques such as pruning, quantization, and knowledge distillation can reduce the size and complexity of models while maintaining accuracy. Smaller models require less computational power, enabling faster inference.

2. TensorRT: TensorRT is a high-performance deep learning inference optimizer and runtime developed by NVIDIA. It can significantly improve inference speed on NVIDIA GPUs by optimizing models for specific hardware and applying techniques such as layer fusion and precision calibration.

3. ONNX: The Open Neural Network Exchange (ONNX) is an open-source format for representing machine learning models. It allows for interoperability between different frameworks and can be used to optimize models for deployment across various environments.

Using a Model Serving Framework

Model serving frameworks streamline the process of deploying and managing machine learning models in production. Some popular options include:

1. TensorFlow Serving: Designed specifically for serving TensorFlow models, TensorFlow Serving provides a flexible architecture for managing multiple models and versions. It allows for easy integration with existing systems and supports gRPC and REST APIs for serving predictions.

2. Seldon: Seldon is an open-source platform for deploying machine learning models in Kubernetes environments. It provides capabilities for A/B testing, canary releases, and monitoring, making it easier to manage and scale models in production.

Chapter 13: Advanced Techniques in Machine Learning

Introduction to Advanced Machine Learning Techniques

In the rapidly evolving field of machine learning, basic algorithms and models often fall short of addressing complex real-world problems. Advanced techniques are essential for extracting deeper insights from data, improving model performance, and tackling unique challenges. These techniques not only enhance predictive accuracy but also contribute to the interpretability and robustness of machine learning models.

Understanding advanced machine learning techniques involves delving into areas such as ensemble methods, deep learning, transfer learning, reinforcement learning, and unsupervised learning strategies. Each of these areas presents unique approaches to solving intricate problems and can be tailored to specific applications.

By exploring these advanced techniques, practitioners can expand their toolkit, enabling them to tackle a broader range of tasks and optimize their models for better performance in diverse environments.

Ensemble Methods

Ensemble methods combine multiple models to produce a single, more accurate model. This approach capitalizes on the strengths of individual models while mitigating their weaknesses. The underlying principle is that a group of weak learners can collectively create a strong learner. Two primary types of ensemble methods are bagging and boosting.

Bagging (Bootstrap Aggregating)

Bagging aims to reduce variance by averaging predictions from multiple models trained on different subsets of the training data. This technique is particularly useful for high-variance models, such as decision trees. By training multiple models independently, bagging creates a diverse set of predictions.

The most notable bagging algorithm is the Random Forest, which uses multiple decision trees trained on bootstrapped samples of the data. Each tree makes independent predictions, and the final output is obtained by averaging (for regression) or voting (for classification). This approach enhances robustness and reduces the risk of overfitting.

Boosting

Boosting focuses on improving model performance by sequentially training models, where each new model attempts to correct the errors made by its predecessor. This method aims to reduce bias and can effectively turn weak learners into strong learners.

The AdaBoost algorithm is one of the most popular boosting techniques. It assigns weights to each training instance based on the errors made by previous models, allowing subsequent models to focus on the more difficult cases. Another notable boosting method is Gradient Boosting, which builds models in a stage-wise fashion and optimizes a specified loss function.

Both bagging and boosting are powerful techniques that can significantly enhance the performance of machine learning models, making them essential tools in a practitioner's arsenal.

Deep Learning

Deep learning, a subfield of machine learning, involves the use of artificial neural networks with multiple layers to learn representations of data. It has gained prominence due to its ability to automatically extract features from raw data, making it particularly effective for complex tasks such as image recognition, natural language processing, and speech recognition.

Understanding Neural Networks

At the core of deep learning are neural networks, which are inspired by the human brain's structure. A typical neural network consists of layers of interconnected nodes (neurons). Each neuron processes input data, applies a weight and bias, and passes the result through an activation function to introduce non-linearity.

Deep neural networks (DNNs) contain multiple hidden layers, allowing them to learn intricate patterns and representations from data. The training process involves adjusting the weights through backpropagation, minimizing the difference between predicted outputs and actual targets.

Convolutional Neural Networks (CNNs)

CNNs are a specialized type of neural network primarily used for image processing tasks. They utilize convolutional layers that apply filters to the input data, allowing the model to learn spatial hierarchies of features. This architecture is particularly effective for tasks like image classification, object detection, and segmentation.

CNNs also employ pooling layers to reduce dimensionality and improve computational efficiency. Techniques such as data augmentation can be used to enhance training by artificially increasing the diversity of the training dataset.

Recurrent Neural Networks (RNNs)

RNNs are designed for sequential data, making them ideal for tasks such as natural language processing and time series forecasting. Unlike traditional neural networks, RNNs maintain an internal state (memory) that captures information about previous inputs. This allows them to model temporal dependencies and capture patterns over time.

Long Short-Term Memory (LSTM) networks and Gated Recurrent Units (GRUs) are advanced RNN architectures that address issues such as vanishing gradients, enabling the model to learn long-range dependencies more effectively.

Transfer Learning

Transfer learning is a powerful technique that allows practitioners to leverage pre-trained models on new tasks, particularly when data is scarce. By transferring knowledge from a related task, models can achieve higher performance with less training data and time.

Pre-trained Models

In transfer learning, a model trained on a large dataset (such as ImageNet for image classification) is fine-tuned on a smaller, task-specific dataset. The early layers of the model, which capture general features, remain frozen, while the later layers are retrained to adapt to the new task. This process enables practitioners to benefit from the rich representations learned by deep networks without starting from scratch.

Applications of Transfer Learning

Transfer learning is widely applied in various domains, including computer vision, natural language processing, and even healthcare. For instance, in image classification tasks, a pre-trained CNN can be adapted for specific classes with minimal additional data. In NLP, models like BERT and GPT have been trained on vast corpora, and practitioners can fine-tune these models for specific language tasks such as sentiment analysis or named entity recognition.

The effectiveness of transfer learning makes it a valuable approach for practitioners facing data limitations while striving for high model performance.

Reinforcement Learning

Reinforcement learning (RL) is a unique paradigm where agents learn to make decisions by interacting with an environment. Unlike supervised learning, which relies on labeled data, RL agents learn through trial and error, receiving feedback in the form of rewards or penalties.

Core Concepts in Reinforcement Learning

Reinforcement learning involves several key concepts:

- **Agent**: The learner or decision-maker that interacts with the environment.
- **Environment**: The external system that the agent interacts with, providing states and rewards.
- **State**: A representation of the current situation or context in which the agent finds itself.
- **Action**: The choices available to the agent at any given state.
- **Reward**: A feedback signal received after taking an action, indicating the success of the action in achieving the desired goal.

The primary objective of an RL agent is to learn a policy that maximizes cumulative rewards over time. This process involves exploring the environment to discover which actions yield the best rewards while balancing exploration and exploitation.

Popular Algorithms in Reinforcement Learning

Several algorithms are commonly used in reinforcement learning, including:

1. Q-Learning: Q-Learning is a value-based method that seeks to learn the optimal action-value function, which estimates the expected future rewards for taking a given action in a specific state. The agent updates its Q-values based on the rewards received, gradually converging to the optimal policy.

2. Deep Q-Networks (DQN): DQN combines Q-Learning with deep learning, using neural networks to approximate the Q-values. This approach allows agents to handle high-dimensional state spaces, such as images, making it suitable for complex environments.

3. Policy Gradients: Policy gradient methods directly optimize the policy by estimating the gradient of the expected reward with respect to the policy parameters. This approach is effective for continuous action spaces and allows for more expressive policies.

Applications of Reinforcement Learning

Reinforcement learning has found applications in various fields, including robotics, game playing, and recommendation systems. Notable successes include DeepMind's AlphaGo, which defeated world champions in the game of Go, and autonomous vehicles, where RL is used to make real-time navigation decisions.

Unsupervised Learning Strategies

Unsupervised learning techniques focus on discovering patterns and relationships within unlabeled data. Unlike supervised learning, where models are trained on labeled datasets, unsupervised learning aims to find inherent structures in the data.

Clustering

Clustering is a fundamental unsupervised learning technique that groups similar data points based on their features. Popular clustering algorithms include:

- **K-Means**: K-Means partitions data into K clusters by minimizing the variance within each cluster. It is efficient but requires the number of clusters to be specified in advance.

- **Hierarchical Clustering**: Hierarchical clustering builds a tree-like structure of clusters, allowing for a more flexible representation of data relationships. It can be divided into agglomerative and divisive approaches.
- **DBSCAN (Density-Based Spatial Clustering of Applications with Noise)**: DBSCAN identifies clusters based on the density of data points, making it effective for discovering clusters of varying shapes and sizes.

Dimensionality Reduction

Dimensionality reduction techniques are used to reduce the number of features in a dataset while preserving its essential characteristics. This is particularly useful for visualizing high-dimensional data and mitigating the curse of dimensionality.

- **Principal Component Analysis (PCA)**: PCA transforms the data into a lower-dimensional space by identifying the directions (principal components) that maximize variance.
- **t-Distributed Stochastic Neighbor Embedding (t-SNE)**: t-SNE is a nonlinear dimensionality reduction technique that focuses on preserving the local structure of data, making it effective for visualizing clusters in high-dimensional spaces.

Anomaly Detection

Unsupervised learning can also be used for anomaly detection, where the goal is to identify rare events or outliers in the data. Techniques such as Isolation Forests and One-Class SVM are commonly employed for this purpose, helping practitioners identify unusual patterns that may indicate fraud, system failures, or other critical issues.

In , advanced machine learning techniques enable practitioners to address complex problems, enhance model performance, and expand their capabilities. By mastering ensemble methods, deep learning, transfer learning, reinforcement learning, and unsupervised learning strategies, data scientists can unlock new possibilities and

Chapter 14: Practical Applications of Machine Learning

Real-World Applications of Machine Learning

Machine learning has transcended theoretical frameworks and is now a vital tool across various industries. Its applications are as diverse as they are impactful, driving innovation and efficiency in sectors ranging from healthcare to finance. Understanding these applications allows practitioners to see the tangible benefits of machine learning and inspires them to implement solutions in their respective fields.

The breadth of machine learning applications is vast, and they can generally be categorized into several key domains, including predictive analytics, natural language processing (NLP), computer vision, recommendation systems, and robotics. Each of these domains presents unique challenges and opportunities for leveraging machine learning techniques to solve real-world problems.

Predictive Analytics

Predictive analytics involves using historical data to make informed predictions about future events. By employing machine learning algorithms, businesses can gain insights that drive decision-making processes. This application is prevalent in various fields, including finance, marketing, and healthcare.

Finance

In finance, predictive analytics is utilized for credit scoring, risk assessment, and fraud detection. Financial institutions analyze customer data, transaction history, and other relevant information to predict potential defaults on loans or credit cards. Machine learning models can identify patterns associated with fraudulent behavior, enabling timely interventions and reducing losses.

Healthcare

Predictive analytics plays a significant role in healthcare by predicting patient outcomes, hospital readmissions, and disease progression. Machine learning algorithms can analyze electronic health records (EHRs) to identify patients at risk of developing specific conditions. For instance, models can predict the likelihood of a patient being readmitted within a certain timeframe after discharge, allowing healthcare providers to implement preventive measures.

Marketing

In marketing, predictive analytics helps businesses target the right customers at the right time. By analyzing customer behavior and demographics, companies can forecast which customers are likely to convert and tailor marketing campaigns accordingly. This targeted approach improves customer engagement and maximizes return on investment.

Natural Language Processing (NLP)

Natural language processing involves the interaction between computers and human language. Machine learning techniques enable machines to understand, interpret, and generate human language, paving the way for various applications that enhance user experiences and streamline operations.

Chatbots and Virtual Assistants

Chatbots have become an integral part of customer service, providing instant support and assistance to users. By employing NLP techniques, chatbots can understand user queries, analyze intent, and provide relevant responses. They can handle a wide range of inquiries, reducing the need for human intervention and improving response times.

Sentiment Analysis

Sentiment analysis involves determining the sentiment expressed in a piece of text, such as social media posts, product reviews, or customer feedback. By applying machine learning algorithms, businesses can gain insights into customer opinions and sentiments, allowing them to make data-driven decisions regarding product improvements or marketing strategies.

Language Translation

Machine translation systems, such as Google Translate, leverage NLP and machine learning to translate text from one language to another. These systems have improved significantly in recent years, enabling seamless communication across language barriers. By utilizing deep learning techniques, models can capture the nuances of language, resulting in more accurate translations.

Computer Vision

Computer vision is a field that focuses on enabling machines to interpret and understand visual information from the world. Machine learning techniques are fundamental to achieving significant advancements in image and video analysis, leading to a wide array of applications.

Image Classification

Image classification involves assigning a label to an image based on its content. Convolutional Neural Networks (CNNs) are widely used for this task, demonstrating remarkable performance in classifying images across various domains. Applications range from identifying objects in photographs to diagnosing medical conditions through imaging studies.

Facial Recognition

Facial recognition technology utilizes machine learning to identify and verify individuals based on facial features. This application has gained traction in security systems, social media platforms, and mobile devices. By training models on vast datasets of facial images, systems can accurately recognize individuals in real-time, enhancing security and user experience.

Autonomous Vehicles

Machine learning is a cornerstone of autonomous vehicle technology. By processing data from cameras, LIDAR, and other sensors, machine learning algorithms enable vehicles to perceive their surroundings, make decisions, and navigate safely. These systems rely on computer vision techniques to identify objects, road signs, and obstacles, paving the way for safer and more efficient transportation.

Recommendation Systems

Recommendation systems are designed to suggest products, services, or content to users based on their preferences and behavior. By analyzing historical data, machine learning models can predict what users are likely to enjoy, enhancing user satisfaction and driving engagement.

E-Commerce

In e-commerce, recommendation systems play a crucial role in personalizing the shopping experience. By analyzing user behavior, purchase history, and product attributes, platforms like Amazon can suggest relevant products to users. This targeted approach not only increases sales but also improves customer retention.

Streaming Services

Streaming platforms such as Netflix and Spotify leverage recommendation systems to curate personalized content for users. By analyzing viewing or listening habits, these platforms can suggest movies, shows, or songs that align with users' preferences. This personalization enhances user engagement and keeps subscribers coming back for more.

Social Media

Social media platforms utilize recommendation algorithms to curate content for users, determining which posts, pages, or groups to highlight. By analyzing user interactions and preferences, these systems enhance user experience and keep users engaged with the platform.

Robotics

Machine learning has become increasingly important in the field of robotics, enabling machines to learn from data and adapt to their environments. This application of machine learning extends beyond traditional industrial robotics to include autonomous systems, drones, and robotic assistants.

Industrial Automation

In manufacturing, machine learning is used to optimize production processes and enhance efficiency. By analyzing data from sensors and machines, algorithms can identify patterns and anomalies, enabling predictive maintenance and reducing downtime. This data-driven approach enhances operational efficiency and reduces costs.

Drones

Drones equipped with machine learning algorithms can perform various tasks, from aerial surveillance to delivery services. By analyzing data from cameras and sensors, drones can navigate complex environments and make real-time decisions. This capability has applications in agriculture, disaster response, and logistics.

Robotic Assistants

Robotic assistants are increasingly being deployed in healthcare, hospitality, and home environments. By leveraging machine learning, these robots can understand and respond to human interactions, perform tasks, and adapt to changing conditions. For example, robotic companions for the elderly can provide companionship, monitor health, and assist with daily activities.

The practical applications of machine learning are vast and varied, transforming industries and enhancing our daily lives. By understanding how machine learning can be leveraged across different domains, practitioners can identify opportunities to implement innovative solutions that drive efficiency, improve user experiences, and create value. As technology continues to evolve, the potential for machine learning applications will only expand, paving the way for new possibilities and advancements.

Chapter 15: Ethics and Fairness in Machine Learning

Understanding the Importance of Ethics in Machine Learning

As machine learning technologies become increasingly integrated into various aspects of society, the ethical implications of these systems are garnering significant attention. The deployment of machine learning models can have profound effects on individuals, communities, and institutions, making it crucial to consider the ethical dimensions of their use. Ethical machine learning is not merely an optional consideration but a fundamental requirement for ensuring that these technologies contribute positively to society.

The importance of ethics in machine learning arises from the potential for bias, discrimination, and unintended consequences. Machine learning models learn from data, and if that data reflects historical biases or social inequalities, the models may perpetuate or even amplify these issues. Consequently, ethical considerations must guide the development, deployment, and monitoring of machine learning systems to promote fairness, accountability, and transparency.

In this chapter, we will explore the critical aspects of ethics in machine learning, focusing on bias and fairness, accountability in model development, the importance of transparency, and strategies for fostering ethical practices in the machine learning community.

Bias and Fairness in Machine Learning

Bias in machine learning refers to systematic errors that result from prejudiced data or flawed algorithms. These biases can lead to unfair treatment of individuals based on attributes such as race, gender, age, or socioeconomic status. Addressing bias is essential to ensure that machine learning models produce fair outcomes for all users.

Types of Bias

There are several types of bias that can manifest in machine learning models:

- **Data Bias**: Data bias occurs when the training data is unrepresentative or biased in some way. For example, if a facial recognition system is

trained predominantly on images of one demographic group, it may perform poorly on individuals from other groups, leading to discriminatory outcomes.
- **Algorithmic Bias**: Algorithmic bias arises from the design of the algorithms themselves. Certain algorithms may amplify existing biases in the data, resulting in skewed predictions. For instance, if an algorithm is designed to optimize for accuracy without considering fairness, it may favor certain groups over others.
- **Human Bias**: Human bias can be introduced during the data collection, labeling, and model development processes. The choices made by data scientists and engineers can inadvertently reflect societal biases, impacting the final model's behavior.

Assessing Fairness

Fairness in machine learning can be defined in various ways, and different metrics can be employed to assess fairness:

- **Demographic Parity**: This metric requires that the outcomes of a model are independent of protected attributes (e.g., race, gender). For example, in a hiring algorithm, demographic parity would ensure that candidates from

different demographic groups are equally likely to be selected.
- **Equal Opportunity**: Equal opportunity focuses on ensuring that individuals from different groups have equal chances of receiving positive outcomes. In a credit scoring model, this would mean that individuals from minority groups should have the same probability of being approved for loans as those from majority groups, conditional on their creditworthiness.
- **Individual Fairness**: Individual fairness stipulates that similar individuals should be treated similarly. This principle requires a thorough understanding of the context and characteristics of individuals to ensure equitable treatment.

Mitigating Bias

To address bias and promote fairness in machine learning models, several strategies can be employed:

- **Diverse Data Collection**: Ensuring that the training data is diverse and representative of the target population is crucial. This involves actively seeking out underrepresented groups and ensuring their perspectives and characteristics are included.

- **Bias Audits**: Regularly auditing machine learning models for bias can help identify and mitigate unfair outcomes. This can involve testing models on various demographic groups to assess performance disparities and make necessary adjustments.
- **Fairness Constraints**: Incorporating fairness constraints into the model training process can help ensure that models adhere to fairness principles. Techniques such as adversarial debiasing can be employed to penalize biased predictions.
- **Stakeholder Engagement**: Engaging stakeholders throughout the machine learning development process can provide valuable insights into potential biases and fairness concerns. By involving diverse perspectives, practitioners can better understand the implications of their models.

Accountability in Machine Learning

Accountability in machine learning refers to the responsibility of organizations and individuals involved in the development and deployment of models. Establishing accountability is essential to ensure that machine learning systems are used ethically and do not harm individuals or communities.

Establishing Clear Responsibilities

Organizations must define clear roles and responsibilities for individuals involved in the machine learning lifecycle, including data collection, model development, and deployment. This involves creating guidelines that outline the ethical standards and practices that should be followed throughout the process.

Documentation and Traceability

Maintaining thorough documentation of the machine learning process is critical for accountability. This includes documenting data sources, model development choices, and evaluation metrics. Traceability ensures that organizations can track decisions made at various stages and understand the potential impact of their models.

Addressing Unintended Consequences

Machine learning models can have unintended consequences that may not be apparent during development. Organizations must establish processes for monitoring deployed models to identify and address issues as they arise. This involves continuously evaluating model performance and its impact on different demographic groups.

The Importance of Transparency

Transparency in machine learning refers to the clarity and openness of the processes involved in model development, training, and deployment. Transparent practices enhance trust among stakeholders and enable users to understand how decisions are made.

Explainability

Explainability is a crucial aspect of transparency. Users should be able to comprehend how a machine learning model arrived at a particular decision. Techniques such as LIME (Local Interpretable Model-Agnostic Explanations) and SHAP (SHapley Additive exPlanations) can help provide insights into the model's behavior and feature importance.

Open Communication

Organizations should foster open communication with stakeholders, including users, regulators, and affected communities. This involves sharing information about model capabilities, limitations, and potential biases. Transparency allows for informed discussions about the ethical implications of machine learning systems.

Building Trust

Transparent practices contribute to building trust in machine learning systems. When users understand how decisions are made and have confidence in the fairness of the models, they are more likely to embrace these technologies. Trust is essential for the successful integration of machine learning into various applications.

Fostering Ethical Practices in Machine Learning

Promoting ethical practices in machine learning requires a collective effort from practitioners, organizations, and the broader community. By adopting a proactive approach to ethics, the machine learning community can work towards creating systems that are fair, accountable, and transparent.

Education and Training

Education and training programs focused on ethics in machine learning should be developed for practitioners, data scientists, and stakeholders. By increasing awareness of ethical considerations, practitioners can make informed decisions that prioritize fairness and accountability.

Establishing Ethical Guidelines

Organizations should establish clear ethical guidelines for machine learning practices. These guidelines should outline principles related to bias, fairness, transparency, and accountability. Regularly revisiting and updating these guidelines is essential as the field continues to evolve.

Engaging Diverse Perspectives

Engaging diverse perspectives in the machine learning development process can provide valuable insights into ethical considerations. By involving individuals from different backgrounds, organizations can better understand the implications of their models and identify potential biases.

Collaboration and Regulation

Collaboration between academia, industry, and regulatory bodies can help promote ethical practices in machine learning. Establishing frameworks for ethical oversight and regulation can ensure that organizations adhere to responsible practices.

In summary, ethics and fairness in machine learning are critical considerations that must guide the development and deployment of these technologies. By addressing bias, establishing accountability, promoting transparency, and fostering ethical practices, the machine learning community can work towards creating systems that benefit society as a whole. The journey toward ethical machine learning requires ongoing reflection, collaboration, and commitment from all stakeholders involved.

Chapter 16: Machine Learning in Industry

The Role of Machine Learning in Various Industries

Machine learning has become an integral part of modern industries, reshaping processes, enhancing efficiencies, and driving innovation. As organizations strive to stay competitive in a rapidly changing landscape, the adoption of machine learning technologies has emerged as a key differentiator. This chapter explores the diverse applications of machine learning across several key sectors, including finance, healthcare, manufacturing, retail, and transportation.

Understanding how machine learning can be applied within these industries not only highlights its transformative potential but also offers insights into the specific challenges and opportunities that each sector presents. This exploration serves as a guide for practitioners looking to implement machine learning solutions tailored to their industry's needs.

Machine Learning in Finance

The finance industry has been at the forefront of adopting machine learning technologies, leveraging data to optimize decision-making, enhance risk management, and improve customer experiences. Machine learning applications in finance can be categorized into several key areas:

Risk Assessment and Fraud Detection

Machine learning algorithms are widely used for risk assessment in lending and insurance. By analyzing historical data, these models can identify patterns associated with creditworthiness, allowing financial institutions to make informed lending decisions. Similarly, in insurance, machine learning can help in determining premiums based on individual risk profiles.

Fraud detection is another critical application. Financial institutions utilize machine learning to monitor transactions in real-time, identifying suspicious activities and potential fraud attempts. Algorithms can learn from historical fraudulent behavior, allowing them to detect anomalies and flag potentially fraudulent transactions quickly.

Algorithmic Trading

Algorithmic trading involves the use of machine learning models to analyze market data and execute trades at optimal times. By leveraging vast amounts of historical data, these models can identify trading patterns and make predictions about future price movements. This approach can enhance trading strategies, increase profitability, and reduce human error.

Customer Service and Chatbots

Machine learning-powered chatbots have transformed customer service in the finance sector. These chatbots can handle routine inquiries, assist with transactions, and provide personalized recommendations based on customer behavior. By improving response times and enhancing customer experiences, financial institutions can build stronger relationships with their clients.

Machine Learning in Healthcare

The healthcare industry has embraced machine learning to improve patient outcomes, enhance operational efficiency, and drive research advancements. Applications in this sector are diverse and impactful:

Predictive Analytics for Patient Outcomes

Machine learning models are employed to predict patient outcomes, such as hospital readmission rates or the likelihood of disease progression. By analyzing electronic health records (EHRs) and patient histories, these models can identify high-risk patients and enable healthcare providers to implement timely interventions.

Medical Imaging and Diagnostics

In medical imaging, machine learning algorithms are used to analyze images from X-rays, MRIs, and CT scans. Deep learning techniques, particularly convolutional neural networks (CNNs), have demonstrated exceptional performance in diagnosing conditions such as tumors, fractures, and other abnormalities. This technology can enhance diagnostic accuracy and assist radiologists in making more informed decisions.

Drug Discovery and Development

Machine learning is revolutionizing the drug discovery process by predicting the efficacy and safety of potential drug candidates. By analyzing biological data and chemical properties, machine learning models can identify promising compounds for further testing, significantly speeding up the development process and reducing costs.

Personalized Medicine

Personalized medicine leverages machine learning to tailor treatments to individual patients based on their unique genetic profiles and health histories. By analyzing genomic data, clinicians can identify the most effective treatments for specific conditions, improving patient outcomes and minimizing adverse effects.

Machine Learning in Manufacturing

In manufacturing, machine learning is driving innovations in production processes, quality control, and supply chain management. Its applications can enhance efficiency, reduce costs, and improve product quality.

Predictive Maintenance

Machine learning algorithms are used for predictive maintenance, allowing manufacturers to anticipate equipment failures before they occur. By analyzing sensor data from machines, these models can identify patterns indicative of potential failures, enabling timely interventions and minimizing downtime.

Quality Control

Machine learning is applied in quality control processes to identify defects and anomalies in products. By analyzing images and sensor data, algorithms can detect deviations from quality standards, ensuring that only products meeting specifications reach the market.

Supply Chain Optimization

Machine learning enhances supply chain management by predicting demand, optimizing inventory levels, and improving logistics. By analyzing historical sales data and external factors, these models can forecast demand fluctuations, allowing manufacturers to make informed decisions about production and distribution.

Machine Learning in Retail

The retail industry has harnessed machine learning to enhance customer experiences, optimize inventory management, and drive sales. Key applications include:

Personalized Recommendations

Machine learning algorithms power recommendation systems that suggest products to customers based on their browsing and purchase history. By analyzing customer behavior, retailers can deliver personalized shopping experiences, increasing customer satisfaction and driving sales.

Inventory Management

Machine learning helps retailers optimize inventory levels by predicting demand for various products. By analyzing historical sales data, seasonal trends, and external factors, these models enable retailers to maintain optimal stock levels, reducing the risk of overstocking or stockouts.

Customer Segmentation

Retailers utilize machine learning to segment their customer base, identifying distinct groups with similar preferences and behaviors. This segmentation allows for targeted marketing strategies and personalized promotions, increasing engagement and conversion rates.

Machine Learning in Transportation

The transportation industry is experiencing a transformation driven by machine learning technologies. From optimizing logistics to enhancing safety, machine learning applications are reshaping how goods and people move.

Autonomous Vehicles

Machine learning is fundamental to the development of autonomous vehicles. By processing data from cameras,

LIDAR, and sensors, machine learning algorithms enable vehicles to navigate and make decisions in real-time. This technology has the potential to enhance road safety and improve transportation efficiency.

Traffic Prediction and Management

Machine learning models are used to predict traffic patterns and optimize traffic flow in urban areas. By analyzing historical traffic data and real-time conditions, these models can provide insights for city planners and traffic management systems, reducing congestion and improving travel times.

Logistics and Route Optimization

In logistics, machine learning helps optimize delivery routes and reduce transportation costs. By analyzing factors such as traffic conditions, weather, and delivery schedules, these models can recommend the most efficient routes, improving delivery times and reducing fuel consumption.

Machine learning is reshaping industries by providing innovative solutions to complex challenges. From finance and healthcare to manufacturing, retail, and transportation, the applications of machine learning are diverse and impactful. By understanding these applications, practitioners can identify opportunities to implement machine learning technologies that drive efficiency, enhance customer experiences, and foster innovation. As machine learning continues to evolve, its role in transforming industries will only expand, paving the way for new advancements and possibilities.

Chapter 17: Future Trends in Machine Learning

Emerging Technologies and Innovations

As machine learning continues to advance, it is crucial to examine the emerging technologies and trends that will shape its future. The landscape of machine learning is dynamic, influenced by ongoing research, advancements in computational power, and the increasing availability of data. This chapter explores some of the most promising trends in machine learning, including advances in deep learning, the rise of automated machine learning (AutoML), the integration of machine learning with other technologies, and the increasing focus on ethical AI.

Understanding these trends will help practitioners and organizations prepare for the future of machine learning and leverage its full potential in various applications.

Advancements in Deep Learning

Deep learning has been a driving force behind many recent breakthroughs in machine learning. This subset of machine learning, which focuses on neural networks with multiple layers, has led to significant advancements in various fields, including computer vision, natural language processing, and speech recognition.

Transformers and Natural Language Processing

The introduction of transformer models, such as BERT (Bidirectional Encoder Representations from Transformers) and GPT (Generative Pre-trained Transformer), has revolutionized natural language processing. These models leverage attention mechanisms to process and understand context in text, leading to breakthroughs in tasks such as translation, summarization, and question answering.

Future developments in this area are likely to focus on making these models more efficient, reducing their computational requirements while maintaining high performance. Research into model compression techniques, such as knowledge distillation, will play a crucial role in deploying these models in resource-constrained environments.

Generative Models

Generative models, particularly Generative Adversarial Networks (GANs), have gained prominence for their ability to create realistic synthetic data. This technology is being explored in various applications, including image generation, video synthesis, and even music composition. The future will likely see further enhancements in the quality and diversity of generated content, along with applications in creative industries and data augmentation.

Explainable AI

As deep learning models become more complex, the need for explainability grows. Researchers are focusing on developing techniques to provide insights into how models make decisions, aiming to improve transparency and trust in machine learning systems. Future trends will likely emphasize the importance of explainable AI, particularly in high-stakes applications such as healthcare and finance.

Automated Machine Learning (AutoML)

The rise of AutoML is a significant trend aimed at democratizing machine learning by making it accessible to a broader audience, including non-experts. AutoML platforms automate various aspects of the machine learning workflow, from data preprocessing to model selection and hyperparameter tuning.

Simplifying the Workflow

AutoML tools simplify the process of building machine learning models, allowing users to focus on problem formulation rather than the technical intricacies. This trend is likely to continue, with platforms becoming increasingly user-friendly and capable of handling complex tasks.

Integration with Business Processes

As businesses recognize the value of machine learning, AutoML will play a crucial role in integrating machine learning into business processes. By automating model development, organizations can rapidly deploy solutions that address specific business challenges, accelerating the pace of innovation.

Improved Performance through Ensemble Learning

Future developments in AutoML may include advanced ensemble learning techniques that combine the strengths of multiple models to enhance performance. By leveraging diverse algorithms and architectures, these systems can improve accuracy and robustness while reducing overfitting.

Integration with Other Technologies

The integration of machine learning with other emerging technologies is another trend that will shape its future. By combining machine learning with technologies such as the Internet of Things (IoT), edge computing, and blockchain, new applications and capabilities will emerge.

Internet of Things (IoT)

The proliferation of IoT devices generates vast amounts of data, creating opportunities for machine learning to analyze and derive insights from this information. Future trends will likely focus on real-time analytics, enabling organizations to make data-driven decisions based on the continuous stream of data from connected devices.

Edge Computing

Edge computing, which involves processing data closer to its source, is set to enhance the deployment of machine learning applications in real-time scenarios. By reducing latency and bandwidth requirements, edge computing enables machine learning models to operate efficiently in applications such as autonomous vehicles and smart cities.

Blockchain and Data Integrity

Blockchain technology presents opportunities for enhancing data integrity and security in machine learning. By leveraging decentralized ledgers, organizations can ensure the authenticity of training data and improve trust in machine learning models. Future developments may explore how machine learning can be integrated with blockchain to create transparent and auditable systems.

Focus on Ethical AI

As machine learning becomes increasingly embedded in society, the focus on ethical AI is paramount. Organizations and researchers are recognizing the need to develop responsible and fair machine learning systems that prioritize transparency, accountability, and inclusivity.

Addressing Bias and Fairness

Future trends will likely emphasize the importance of addressing bias in machine learning models. Researchers will continue to explore methodologies for mitigating bias during data collection, model training, and evaluation. This includes developing frameworks for auditing machine learning systems to ensure fairness and equity.

Regulation and Governance

With growing concerns about the ethical implications of AI, regulatory frameworks are likely to emerge to govern the use of machine learning technologies. Organizations will need to adapt to these regulations, ensuring compliance while fostering ethical practices in machine learning development.

Human-Centered AI

The future of machine learning will increasingly focus on human-centered AI, prioritizing user needs and values in the design and deployment of systems. This approach emphasizes collaboration between humans and machines, ensuring that AI technologies augment human capabilities rather than replace them.

The future of machine learning is characterized by exciting advancements and emerging trends that will shape its applications and impact on society. From breakthroughs in deep learning to the rise of AutoML and the integration with other technologies, machine learning will continue to evolve and play a crucial role across various industries. As practitioners navigate this landscape, an emphasis on ethical AI and responsible practices will be essential to ensure that machine learning technologies contribute positively to society. Preparing for these trends will empower organizations to leverage the full potential of machine learning while addressing the challenges and responsibilities that come with it.